Pioneering

OREGON ARCHITECT
W.D. PUGH

Pioneering
OREGON ARCHITECT
W.D. PUGH

TERENCE EMMONS

THE
History
PRESS

Published by The History Press
Charleston, SC
www.historypress.com

Copyright © 2021 by Terence Emmons
All rights reserved

First published 2021

Manufactured in the United States

ISBN 9781467148863

Library of Congress Control Number: 2021931137

Notice: The information in this book is true and complete to the best of our knowledge. It is offered without guarantee on the part of the author or The History Press. The author and The History Press disclaim all liability in connection with the use of this book.

All rights reserved. No part of this book may be reproduced or transmitted in any form whatsoever without prior written permission from the publisher except in the case of brief quotations embodied in critical articles and reviews.

This book is dedicated to the memory of Jessie Hobson Pugh (1880–1983),
Katherine Pugh Schwabauer (1903–2010)
and Mildred Pugh Emmons (1908–1985).

CONTENTS

SEARCHING FOR WALTER PUGH

The earliest memories I have of my grandfather Walter Pugh, who was born in 1863, the year of President Lincoln's Emancipation Proclamation, are all linked to three places. First, and primarily, they are linked to our family home in Salem, on a hilltop couple of acres up Hoyt Street, behind the Pioneer and City View Cemeteries. Next, they are linked to my grandparents' house on North Eighteenth Street (441), a duplex Walter had built in 1921. I remember sitting with him toward the end of the war in the living room there, listening to Gabriel Heatter on the evening news. On the wall above the big console radio were framed portraits of FDR and Stalin (the latter was a *Life* magazine cover photograph from March 1943). And, finally, they are connected to a small house near Monroe, without plumbing or running water (there was a hand pump on the kitchen sink), where I spent part of one summer with my grandparents. Mostly, my memories are centered on 300 Hoyt Street, where our live-in grandparents looked after four small boys during the last couple of years of the war while their father was serving as a naval officer in the Pacific theater (hence the interest of an eight or nine-year-old in the evening news) and their mother worked nights at the Southern Pacific depot in Salem.

Our grandfather Walter Pugh died in 1946 at the age of eighty-three. We all knew that he had been an architect and eventually even became aware of a few of his creations, like the Salem City Hall, which came into the news in connection with an unsuccessful campaign to prevent its demolition in 1972, or the "Whitespires" church in Albany, the subject of a successful restoration campaign some years later to which my wife, Victoria, and I made a modest contribution. But we were not aware of much else. As late as the early 2000s, we toured the Thos. Kay Woolen Mill building across from Willamette University with a friend who was visiting from France, in blissful ignorance that it had been designed by W.D. Pugh in 1896.

Years passed. Then, in the spring of 2019, our son Joseph, Walter Pugh's great-grandson, suggested we organize a tour of "Grandpa Pugh's buildings" for our grandchildren when school let out for summer vacation. Readily agreeing with that fine idea, I turned to the internet to inform myself of "Grandpa's buildings." Now, a year later, the list of buildings that W.D. Pugh either designed or built contains over sixty items and is possibly still growing—a hotel in Dallas, built in 1888, made it onto the list only a few weeks ago.

Murphy, Oregon
June 2020

∽⦇∞⦈⦈

THE FOLLOWING ACCOUNT OF buildings designed or built by W.D. Pugh, accompanied wherever possible by photographs, is dedicated to preserving an extraordinary architectural legacy: the work of Walter David Pugh.

The author's royalties from this publication will be donated to the Historic Photographs Collections of the Salem Public Library, Salem, Oregon.

NOTE TO THE READER

All references to the *Statesman Journal* point to the historical newspaper the *Statesman*, founded by Asahel Bush, not to the current product of the 1980 merger of the *Statesman* and the *Capital Journal* that bears that name. Newspapers.com, used by the author to access historical newspaper material, apparently chose that single designation to deal with slight variations over time on the *Statesman*'s masthead (*Oregon Statesman, Daily Oregon Statesman,* et cetera). *Caveat lector!*

ACKNOWLEDGEMENTS

I would like to express my thanks to the following individuals, who generously helped this latecomer to the history of Oregon architecture in ways both great and small:

Kylie Pine, Elisabeth Walton Potter, Kirsten Straus, Jerry Lomas, Bette Jo Lawson, Robert Olguin, Anna Dvorak, Ariel Valdiva, Stephenie Flora, Brandi Oswald, Cheryl Roffe, Larry Landis, Liz Carter, Edward Teague, Kimberli Fitzgerald, Meredith Doviak, Deb Meaghers, Mary Gallagher, Daniel Murphy, Theresa Rea, Dale Greenley, Dave Hegeman, Natalie Brant, Chris Petersen, Peter Hatch, Tammy Wild, Karen Emmons, Daniel Emmons. Victoria Emmons, Joseph Emmons, Robert Warren, Julia Simic, Jeff Sageser and Laurie Krill.

A LIFE IN BUILDINGS

On March 1, 1885, page 5 of the *Portland Oregonian* carried this notice: "Walter Pugh, an old Salem boy who has been engaged in business for some time, will soon locate in Salem and establish an architect's office." It was to be a remarkable career of architectural activity.

Pugh is probably best known for designing five buildings, four of which are still standing as of this writing: the Shelton-McMurphey-Johnson house in Eugene, Oregon (1887–88); the Thomas Kay Woolen Mill in Salem, Oregon (1896); the Crook County Courthouse in Prineville, Oregon (1906–8); and the bank building in Independence, Oregon (1891). The first two buildings are now museums, while the third is still a functioning courthouse; the fourth has operated continuously as a bank since it first opened. The fifth, the Salem City Hall (1893–96), was demolished in 1972, although it was, at that time, still structurally sound and serving its original purpose.

These five buildings represent the variety of W.D. Pugh's architecture and its geographic scope, but they amount to only a fraction of the public buildings, commercial buildings and private structures he designed over the nearly twenty years between 1886 and 1909. And then there was his work as a builder. All this came into view gradually and, at times, painstakingly, as the search progressed beyond those few relatively well-known buildings.

These pages document, with photographic images in most cases, the remarkable architectural career of Walter Pugh, a large part of which had previously been undocumented and largely unknown. If this is true about much of the architectural legacy of Walter Pugh, it is even more the case with his work as a builder, which is also documented here.

Opposite, top: Shelton McMurphey Johnson House, Eugene, Oregon (1887–88). Shelton McMurphey Johnson House (3) *(www.flickr.com/photos/discoveroregon/29861124815), by Rick Obst, copied by (www.creativecommons.org/licenses/by2.0/deed.en) license.*

Opposite, bottom: Thos. Kay Woolen Mill, Salem, Oregon (1896). *Courtesy of the Oregon State Archives.*

Above: Independence City Bank building, Independence, Oregon (1891). *Courtesy of the Salem Public Library, Historic Photograph Collections, Ben Maxwell, 6272.*

In this endeavor, a significant amount of information about Walter Pugh's life and circumstances—his family history, financial matters, political affiliation and other aspects of his life—came to the foreground. A goal of this exercise in the first place was to learn more about his life, especially the years of his active professional career as architect and builder,

Above: Crook County Courthouse, Prineville, Oregon (1908). *File licensed under GNU Free Documentation License.*

Right: Salem City Hall (1897). *Courtesy of the State Library of Oregon, resource 20060010905-21.jpg.*

by looking at the evidence of the work itself in the almost total absence of written and narrative sources and the disappearance of family members and others who knew him well enough to provide answers to questions about that period of his life.

In looking at this work, two questions stand out. How could it be that most of this legacy apparently remained unknown, even to members of his immediate family, including his two daughters from his second marriage? And why did his architectural career essentially end in 1909, the year he had been deemed "Salem's leading architect" by a local newspaper? These questions and more will be addressed, if not definitively resolved, in the following pages that are dedicated to the life and legacy of Walter D. Pugh.

In generic terms, therefore, this book is a hybrid—neither a study of a regional architect's oeuvre in the context of late nineteenth- and early twentieth-century architectural trends in this country and abroad nor a straightforward biography of "the life and times of" variety. And it is certainly not a psychobiography.

"A life in buildings?"

1

THE MAKING OF AN OREGON ARCHITECT

Walter David Pugh was born in 1863, the unforgettable year of the Emancipation Proclamation, to two pioneer immigrants to the Willamette Valley, David Hall Pugh and Catherine Entz. Theirs are two remarkable stories.

David Hall's journey to Oregon was a classic pioneer tale: overland by wagon as member of an extended, multigenerational family with all their earthly goods and livestock. He came in the great land rush that began in the early 1840s, once wagon travel across the Rocky Mountains, through South Pass, had been demonstrated feasible and well before Oregon Territory officially became incorporated into the United States. In 1843, a group of settlers met at Champoeg, a meeting that led to the creation of a "provisional government of Oregon" and its declaration that White male U.S. citizens, with their wives, were entitled to 620 acres, an act confirmed and made official by the Oregon Donation Land Act of 1850. In that same year, 1843, a wagon train of more than eight hundred people made the overland journey to Oregon. The number rose to two thousand the next year. In 1845, the estimated number of immigrants to Oregon Territory, mainly farmers who were headed for the widely touted agricultural potential of the Willamette Valley, ranges from two thousand to three thousand. Most had set out from St. Joseph or Independence, Missouri.

The Pugh family was part of the 1845 St. Joseph Company train. The patriarch of the family, Reverend William David Pugh, was born in either 1785 or 1790; his place of birth, usually given as South Carolina, was more likely somewhere in Wales.[1] In any case, his was a rather typical story of continual movement westward from the Eastern Seaboard to new frontiers. His children from his first wife, Sarah White (1790–1814), were born in Tennessee, her place of birth. Widower Pugh married his second wife, Janette Donaldson (1795 or 1798–1870), who was also from Tennessee. They moved to Indiana no later than 1818.[2] Their children, including David Hall and nine siblings, were all born in several counties of Indiana. The family moved to Little Rock, Arkansas, in 1836, before moving to Missouri a year or two before joining the 1845 train bound for the Willamette Valley.

David Hall, with his twin sister, Amanda, both survived the journey, eleven-year old David, according to family lore, walking with the oxen most of the way. The family as a whole, however, suffered numerous losses on the trip. "Before they reached Salem, Oregon, their destination, his father, [younger] brother Andy and a little sister, as well as his brother William's wife and two children, died from illnesses contracted on the way."[3] Patriarch William David and the brother and sister did make it to Willamette Valley before succumbing to "mountain fever" in their first winter at Forest Grove. The rest of the family was reunited on land grants on the Willamette River, just north of Salem, by 1847. David's older brother, the just-widowed William Porter, who captained the family train, had gone ahead in 1845 to this area that eventually came to be known as Keizer (after the name *Keizur* of the first pioneer family to settle there, in 1842).[4]

Shortly after the family's arrival, two of David's brothers, William and Silas, left to join the militia of settlers that had formed to fight in the Cayuse War, which had been set off by the Whitman Massacre near Walla Walla on the Columbia River in November 1847.[5] David, too young to join, stayed home "and split rails," but in 1849, all four brothers departed for the California gold fields, along with practically every able-bodied White man in the Willamette Valley. The three older brothers returned to their farms in 1851, while David stayed on to mind their claims until 1853, according to one obituary.[6] According to an obituary in another Salem newspaper, he then spent several years mining gold in southern Oregon, returning to Salem in 1857.[7]

In any event, by about that time, David was learning the carpenter's trade in the employ of A.W. Ferguson, a well-known contractor of the day. He soon became a builder in his own right and is sometimes called "builder and architect" in the papers—although it is doubtful that he had any formal preparation as architect. He was described in Sarah Hunt Steeves's *Remembrance* as "one of Salem's foremost contractors and builders

[who] left many beautiful monuments to his handicraft."[8] The Cumberland Presbyterian Church and the Presbyterian church in Salem are credited to him. His most impressive achievement as a builder was the Cooke-Patton three-and-a-half-story Victorian mansion on Court Street, near the state capitol, which he built in 1869 for one of Salem's most prominent families.[9] He continued as a contractor until shortly before his death, although he was apparently in poor health for several years prior.

Little can be said about David Hall Pugh's education. We know that after his return to Salem, he received some tutoring from Reverend F.S. Hoyt, who, in 1850, had been appointed president of the Oregon Institute, a school for the basic education of the children of Methodist missionaries and local settlers. Hoyt then became president of Wallamet University, which was officially chartered by the territorial legislature in 1853. As late as academic year 1863–64, David Hall's name appears in the university catalogue in a list of students in the "Academical Department," presumably the heir to the institute, which the university ran to prepare students for the collegiate program proper.[10]

On October 24, 1860, David Hall Pugh and Catherine Entz were married, with Reverend Hoyt officiating. The pair may have met at Willamette, where Catherine also took some courses for a time before the public school system got under way, or they may have met at the home of A.W. Ferguson, David's employer, where Catherine was staying.

The story of Catherine's journey to Salem is, if anything, more remarkable than that of her spouse. Her parents, Eneas and Catherine (Rosenberg) Entz, were natives of Alsace ("during the French occupation," as Catherine would pointedly say, according to family lore) who made their way across the Atlantic Ocean and up the Mississippi River to Missouri in 1840. Catherine was born on February 11, 1840, in either Jefferson City or St. Louis. With the discovery of gold in California in 1849, Catherine's older brother, Eneas Jr., packed his horse and left for California. Catherine's father, getting word of some success there, followed him in 1851. Before long, discouraged on the gold front and attracted by the newly proclaimed availability of free land in Oregon, the father and son moved north and took up claims on Thomas Creek in Linn County, some twenty miles southeast of Salem. The son, dispatched back to Missouri to bring out the rest of the family, died soon after his arrival there. Unable to contact her husband, Catherine's mother decided, with the help of her brother-in-law, another Alsatian immigrant living nearby, to take the water route to Oregon, down the Mississippi River, across the isthmus of Panama and up the Columbia River, to the Willamette with their five remaining children. They embarked on their journey in 1851. Catherine was eleven years old.

On their harrowing trip across the isthmus in Panama, Catherine's mother contracted yellow fever and died shortly after arriving in Panama City. The children were befriended by a good Samaritan, who booked them passage on the next boat to San Francisco. There, they were transferred to the boat of Captain Bennett, who happened to own a hotel in Salem, so they were transferred on arrival in Oregon City to a boat bound for Salem. By that time, several—and possibly all—of the children had broken out with the measles and had to be carried aboard on litters. The oldest child on the journey was a fifteen-year-old boy, the youngest was a two-year-old girl. The children spent five weeks at the Bennetts' Hotel before a man showed up there who happened to be their father's neighbor on his claim in Linn County. Word swiftly got to the incredulous father that his children, without their mother, had arrived in Salem, and they were reunited. One of the five children fell ill and died shortly after being reunited with her father. "Thus, were four little lads buried in France, the big capable brother in Missouri, the dear, heartsick mother in Panama and, lastly, the little sister Rachel in Salem."[11]

The three surviving girls were placed in several homes; Catherine, as mentioned, after a short stay with a family near Corvallis, came to live with the Fergusons, where she remained until her marriage in 1860. Catherine's father, with his son, returned to his claim in Linn County and spent some time in southern Oregon, then in the Corvallis area and finally settled near Salem. It is said that he gained a reputation in orchard and vineyard development in Marion County. He never lived with his daughters in a family setting before his death in 1879.[12]

So, architect Walter David Pugh, not unlike many other Salemites of his generation, was a child of pioneers. Both of his maternal grandparents were born in France, and his paternal grandfather was a Welshman. Both of his parents arrived in the Willamette Valley as eleven-year-olds at the end of difficult journeys that cost the lives of numerous family members.[13] And both had ties to Willamette University at the very beginning of its existence.

What we know of Walter's education can be neatly summed up—and nearly exhausted—by this paragraph in his obituary, which appeared in a Salem paper the day after his death in 1946:

Pugh was born in a small house on the corner of Winter and Union Streets April 4, 1863, of David H. and Catherine Pugh, and attended

Left: W.D. Pugh, photograph portrait (circa 1896). *Courtesy of the Oregon Historical Society Research Library, OHS I.D. 0180G074.*

Above: Advertisement, W.D. Pugh, architect. *L.W. Gentry, book and job printer, 1892, courtesy of the University of Oregon Design Library, pna 21502/In C/1.0/.*

Prof. Selwood's private school and Willamette University. He received architectural training while he was in apprenticeship to the architectural firm of McCall [McCaw] and Wickersham, after which he set up his own firm in Salem.[14]

J.A. Selwood, a Willamette alumnus, opened a "select school" with about forty pupils at the beginning of September 1875.[15] In the Willamette University catalog of 1880–81, Walter D. Pugh's name is listed under "Students in Business Course." And in the following 1881–82 catalog, he is listed under "Art Students," along with thirty-two others, mostly men and mostly locals. He was the only student enrolled in "Architectural Drafting."[16] The authoritative source on early Oregon architects informs us that William F. McCaw (1850–1923), a Scotch-Irish emigrant from Belfast to Portland by way of Toronto in 1882, was a very experienced draftsman who partnered, for a brief time, from 1884 to 1885, with Albert Wickersham in a Portland architectural firm where Walter Pugh served as an apprentice.[17] On March 1, 1885, this small item appeared on page 5 of the *Oregonian*: "Walter Pugh, an old Salem boy who has been engaged in business in Portland for some time, will soon locate in Salem and establish an architect's office."

2

OFF AND RUNNING

1885–1900

How does a twenty-two-year-old, fresh out of an apprenticeship, establish an architect's office? The answer, in this case, is that he joined as junior partner with an established architect/builder who was about to retire.

Wilbur F. Boothby was born in Maine in 1840. After attending Fulton College in New York and working for a time as a carpenter and joiner, at the age of twenty-one, he answered the call of the West via the isthmus of Panama, spent some time mining in northern California and then moved on to Salem, Oregon, in 1864.[18] By the 1880s, Boothby had become a prominent citizen of Salem; he was the owner of considerable real estate, including the premises of the newspaper that included his name in a list of the county's biggest property owners.[19] He had worked as foreman in a sash and door factory before opening a factory of his own with a pair of partners. For a time, he had a dry goods store. He then went into construction with one of his factory partners and quickly became Salem's leading building contractor.

Boothby was engaged in several of the largest Salem building projects of the 1870s and 1880s, including the elaborate Renaissance-style Marion County Courthouse, which was completed in 1873.[20] His firm was involved in several major state projects, including the later stages of construction of the second state capitol building and the building of the state penitentiary and the state insane asylum (Oregon State Hospital). The last two institutions were moved to Salem from Portland in conformance with the state constitution, which mandated their location in the capital city. These buildings continued to be expanded and added on to for years to come; the great, 187-foot-tall dome of the capitol building, which had been occupied since 1876, was only placed in 1893. Boothby's involvement in these projects was sometimes described as "supervising architect," but he was principally a builder. Although he apparently had no formal architectural training, he is credited with participating in the design of the first state hospital building.[21]

In 1879, apparently "owing to failing health," Boothby sold his interest in the sash and door company and opened an architect's office.[22] On August 28, 1885, the *Statesman Journal* carried the following announcement on page 3: "Bids are being taken for construction of additional shops on the grounds of Oregon State Penitentiary. Plans and specifications to be seen at the office of Boothby & Pugh, Architects, Salem, Oregon."

We have no details on how the young Walter Pugh came to be junior partner of Wilbur Boothby in his architectural office. Salem was still a small town. Boothby must have been well acquainted with the already long-established fellow contractor David Hall Pugh, Walter's father and the builder of the Cooke mansion, a Salem landmark located a stone's throw from the new capitol building. David Hall Pugh was also more than likely a customer of Boothby's sash and door factory. Walter's skill as a draftsman, soon to be demonstrated in his own projects, would have been seen as a significant addition to the firm's assets.

Then, in 1886, Boothby retired, leaving "W.D. Pugh, Architect" as a solo operation. The short-lived Boothby connection was of considerable importance for the launching of Walter Pugh's career as architect. For one thing, it seems he inherited ongoing construction projects for the State of Oregon from Boothby.[23] In April 1887, Pugh was appointed "architect, having supervision of the construction of the proposed new wing of the asylum [state hospital] by the asylum board." As if in anticipation of queries about giving such an assignment to a person who was so young, the asylum board added to its announcement: "Mr. Pugh, although a young architect, nevertheless has had considerable experience in his profession, and his qualifications fit him for the responsible position for which he has been chosen."[24] In March 1888, Pugh was reportedly working on the plans for a new brick building at the penitentiary, for which a $6,000 appropriation had been made. Later in the same year, it was said he was designing a new steel fence and hydraulic gate for the penitentiary, as well as making plans and specifications for a water tower and tank there. In 1891, there were more cells to be designed, and in 1892, there were even more.

Oregon State Penitentiary, 1892. *Courtesy of the Oregon State Archives.*

It may be that by this time, Pugh had already been designated "state architect," a title he appears to have held for the duration of Democratic governor Sylvester Pennoyer's two-term tenure in office (1887–95). At the time, the title was informal and simply meant that its occupant was the state's default architect for building projects. Perhaps Pugh was consulted for various state projects. (Only many years later, in 1913, was the title made official, to the extent that the state board "relevant to the construction of public buildings" decided to hire State Architect William Knighton for an annual salary of $3,500. He was to have charge of all the architectural work of the state. This position, however, was never made the subject of statute.)[25]

By 1888, Pugh was listed as a member of a precinct committee for a faction of the Democratic Party and as a delegate to the state primary convention (he was also listed as a delegate of the "anti-fusion" faction of the party in 1894).[26] In 1888, he was a member of the wing of the party that was led by Asahel Bush, the sometime publisher of the *Statesman*, a leading figure in the early history of the party and one of Pugh's main clients in the commercial blocks building boom of 1889–91. (See page 49.) One can imagine that his party affiliation, at the very least, did him no harm there or in his ability to win state projects.

In any event, orders for designing buildings and additions for state institutions continued to come to Pugh's office to the century's end and beyond. (See appendix A.) These orders were not only for additions to the penitentiary and insane asylum, but also for improvements to the state fairgrounds and buildings at the State Soldiers' Home near Roseburg, and at the Agricultural College.

On August 19, 1887, the *Weekly Oregon Statesman* ran an article on the August 17 laying of the cornerstone at the new building of the State

Agricultural College near Corvallis: "Interesting Ceremonies. Collation and Speeches—The Full Proceedings, and List of Articles Deposited." Many visitors from Salem and prominent persons from around the state attended the ceremony. The laying of the stone by the Masons was followed by the procession of the Knights Templar and Grand Lodge Masons headed by the Corvallis band. Then came the program: music by the band, a prayer by Reverend J.R.N. Bell, a song by the choir, a historical essay by M.L. Pipes and then more songs, prayer and music. Finally, a "fine address" by the superintendent of public instruction E.B. McElroy on the subject of "industrial education." Then the assemblage adjourned to the Corvallis City Hall to a "beautiful and bountiful collation" spread for 250 by "the ladies of Corvallis." There, more speeches were made by Governor Pennoyer and a number of other prominent Oregonians. Finally, there came a list of articles deposited in the cornerstone. "The building was planned by Walter Pugh of Salem, architect, to cost $20,000, $3,000 more being subscribed." The imposing three-story structure, surmounted by a large clock tower,

The administration building (now Benton Hall) and the station building (now the women's center), at the Oregon Agricultural College (Oregon State University), Corvallis, Oregon (1887 and 1891, respectively). *Courtesy of Harriet's Collection, Oregon State University Special Collections and Archives Research Center, Oregon State University Libraries, Historical Images of Oregon State University, I.D. HC0040.*

Benton Hall (administration building), Oregon Agricultural College, Corvallis, Oregon (1887). *By Bspirek0 (www.creativecommons.org/publicdomain/zero/1.0/deed.en) license.*

probably qualified as an example of the late Victorian Italianate style that was still in vogue in the United States in the 1880s.[27] Originally known as the administration building, it is now called Benton Hall and is the oldest building on the campus of Oregon State University.

In 1891, Pugh designed two more buildings for the agricultural college: the large students' boarding hall, initially named Cauthorn Hall, then Kidder Hall and, presently, Fairbanks Hall. The call for bids for the construction of the student dormitory went out on June 13, 1891. "Drawings and specifications may be seen at the office of W.D. Pugh, Architect, Salem, Oregon."[28] The large, three stories and mansard building with the inevitable surrogate for an Italianate bell tower—in this case, a kind of observation deck with peaked roof—has conserved the exterior lines of the original structure (the "observation deck" has been removed) and is still functioning as a university building. The second, a cottage-sized single-story building, was the station building, or chemical laboratory. A call for bids for its immediate construction, "according to plans and specifications prepared by Mr. W.D. Pugh, architect," was printed in the *Corvallis Gazette-Times* on August 7, 1891. The design of the more imposing, three-story building of Mechanical Hall (1889) has also been attributed to Pugh.[29] The mansard roofline and tall, severely rectangular windows of the 1893–94 addition echo the features of Cauthorn Hall. This complex burned down in 1898.

Cauthorn Hall (1891), Oregon Agricultural College, Corvallis, Oregon. *Courtesy of the Oregon State University Special Collections and Archives Research Center, Oregon State University Libraries, I.D. HC0043.*

OAC Station Building (1891), Oregon Agricultural College, Corvallis, Oregon. *Courtesy of the Oregon State University Special Collections and Archives Research Center, Oregon State University Libraries, Historical Images of Oregon State University, I.D. PO250001.*

Mechanical Hall (1893) Oregon Agricultural College, Corvallis, Oregon. *Courtesy of the Oregon State University Special Collections and Archives Research Center, Oregon State University Libraries, OSU Chronological History, I.D. HC0063.*

Oregon Agricultural College buildings: (*center*) horticultural (poultry) building (1894) and (*background, with tower*) Cauthorn Hall. *Courtesy of the Oregon State University Special Collections and Archives Research Center, Oregon State University Libraries, Historical Images of Oregon State University, I.D. P090:0066.*

For Pugh, his final job of the Pennoyer era of construction at the Oregon Agricultural College was the design of the industrial-style horticulture building. It is still standing off campus, having been completely redesigned by John Bennes in 1913.[30]

Other state projects came to Pugh's office early on; several appear to have been directly inherited from Boothby's shop. These included the design and supervision of the construction ("architect having supervision of the construction") of the new insane asylum wing mentioned previously and for the penitentiary a new brick building (with an estimated cost of $6,000), gates and fencing, a water tower and tank and "24 double iron cells and 32 single iron cells" in 1891 and again in 1892.[31]

Pugh's last significant engagement in a State of Oregon project during the tenure of Governor Pennoyer involved the great dome that was placed on the second state capitol building in 1893. The building had been designed by the Portland architectural firm J.F. Krumbein and W.G. Gilbert in 1873. The building, without the dome, was occupied by state officials in 1876.

The cost of the building at that point was $190,927. In 1888, porticos with Corinthian columns were added at a cost of $100,000. And, finally, the great dome (187 feet high on a 75-foot-tall structure) was added in 1893. The board of capitol building commissioners (the governor, the secretary of state and the state treasurer) awarded its construction to the Portland Bridge and Building Company (with a bid of $42,275). The installation was performed by Western Ironworks of San Francisco.[32] When preparations for the dome's construction and installation began, Krumbein was dismissed from the project by the board of commissioners "because of alleged structural oversights which added to the cost of erecting the dome, although the dome was constructed essentially as Krumbein's firm had designed it."[33]

The question of Walter Pugh's involvement in the dome project must be raised because in a number of reputable sources, he is simply identified, by default (that is, for lack of specificity), as the architect-designer of the dome.[34] However, no contemporary newspaper accounts mention Pugh in that role, nor was he a member of the board of commissioners. More likely than not, the chronicler of early Oregon architects had it right when he wrote in the article devoted to Pugh that "he supervised construction of the dome of the

Oregon Capitol (1876 and 1893). *Courtesy of the Oregon Historical Society Research Library (OrHi 62727).*

Patton postcard photograph. (*On left, with a tower*) Cooke-Patton house, (*on right*) state capitol dome. *Courtesy of the Salem Public Library, Historic Photograph Collections, Salem, I.D. pcjg02.*

old state capitol, completed in 1893."[35] In other words, the state architect took over the role of the dismissed Krumbein. It is possible that Pugh did design the cupola that surmounted the dome, as it was not included as part of the Krumbein-designed dome proper. That capitol building burned down on April 25, 1935.

Pugh's work on projects for the State of Oregon continued after Pennoyer's tenure as governor ended and, indeed, well after the turn of the century. But practically from the beginning, he was also designing city halls, school buildings, post offices, commercial buildings—mainly in downtown Salem, but also in other towns—a factory (woolen mill) and private residences. At the same time, he was continuing and expanding his activity as a contractor.

CITY HALLS

On the same day it carried an appeal for bids on the college chemical lab, August 8, 1891, the *Corvallis Gazette-Times* announced, "Mr. Pugh...has just finished plans for the new city hall to be erected here. The building will be 55 x 75 feet, two stories and mansard, with a bell tower. The front will be pressed brick, trimmed with cut stone, while the entire building will be finished in modern style with all the latest improvements."[36] The high Victorian Italianate Corvallis City Hall was completed in 1892. It was demolished in the 1950s.

A much more ambitious city hall project was undertaken in the capital city of Salem. On March 23, the *Statesman Journal* reported that the city council would hold a special meeting that evening to consider, as a committee of the whole, the designs for a building to be erected on the southwest corner of High and Chemeketa Streets "that will be at once imposing and of sufficient amplitude to be of service for years to come." Several Salem architects had come forth with elaborate plans.

The architects who came forward at this meeting were W.D. Pugh and Charles F. Burggraf.[37] Both submitted fairly detailed descriptions of the plans they were working on. A third declared contender, C.S. McNally, failed to attend.[38] Pugh outlined, in considerable detail, a plan for a building that was 68 by 120 feet, with a 15-foot-high stone basement and two floors above (altogether 81 feet high); a 25-by-25-foot, 150-foot-tall tower on the northeast corner; and a shorter tower on the southeast corner. All of the structure above the basement was to be constructed with pressed brick, terra-cotta and stone, "in classic style of architecture." Details of the interior arrangement of city offices were as follows:

> *The recorder's office will be located in the tower on the first or basement floor with an entrance on the east and one on the north.... To the right of the consultation room is the marshal's office, which opens into the jail at the rear, where thirty-six cells in double tiers are provided. South of the recorder's office and located in the southeast tower is the police court. To the right of the marshal's office is the fire department. The hook-and-ladder truck coming first, then the two engines and the hose wagon all opening onto the street. Back and south of these are the stalls for the horses.* [Quarters for the firemen], *eight bedrooms, a sitting room and a bathroom are on the second floor immediately above the fire department.*

The city offices and council chambers were to be on the second floor, and the third floor was to be occupied entirely by an auditorium for one thousand people, a semi-circular gallery and a twenty-four-by-thirty-eight-foot stage. "Ample exits will be made."

Pugh told the council that the entire building could be completely constructed, "with the exception of the second [third] floor," for $35,000. The newspaper article concludes: "The entire plan is neat and of pleasing appearance, substantial looking and commodious."[39] Its appearance could,

Corvallis City Hall (1891). *Courtesy of Harriet's Collection, the Oregon State University Special Collections and Archives Research Center, Oregon State University Libraries, I.D. HC0596.*

in fact, be judged by the "finished elevation already on display in the art window of Geo. F. Smith, on State Street," as a side article in the same issue of the paper informed its readers.

> *An exposition of the professional skill of Mr. Walter D. Pugh, one of the best known of Oregon's young architects....The finished elevation...as it stands, is quite a work of art in itself, but a further scrutiny into the detailed drawings of the proposed structure reveals in a potent way Mr. Pugh's pre-*

eminent faculty of adoption, for the entire compass of the interior seems to have been subjected to one unvarying rule of usefulness, a confessedly popular idea in the construction of public buildings.

After going into some detail, illustrating its application in Pugh's design, the article concludes: "The ornamentation is exquisite in design and very original. Taken altogether, Mr. Pugh's projected plan will meet every possible demand in the way of utility, strength and beauty, and to the enterprising young architect is due the credit of submitting for popular favor one of the most thoroughly up-to-date plans ever seen in Salem."[40]

The article continued: "Architect Chas. F. Burggraf is busily engaged on a building of Moorish design, which is noted for its simplicity and solidity, together with an appearance of rugged massiveness." Close to Pugh's plan in area (64 by 119 feet) and height, with a basement plus two floors, a significantly shorter tower (97 feet) and smaller jail (one cell for women, the journalist notes), the structure was to be built of pressed brick and stone (no terra-cotta). The "Moorish" element in Burggraf's design cannot be perceived in the verbal description of the newspaper article. No elevations appear to have been made available.

Pugh's plans won the "sense of committee" in a vote of seven to two (these two were blank). On the evening of April 4, 1893, the new city hall came up again in a regular meeting of the city council. A champion of architect McNally managed to get the council to consider his plans (his estimate varied from $33,400 to $39,200), and both Pugh and Burggraf were asked to further explain their plans. Questions about the source of funding and about constructing only part of the building—perhaps without the tower—for the time being were raised. Finally, the vote on the adoption of plans was taken and amended so as not to commit the city to build at once; seven votes were cast for Pugh, and one was cast for McNally.[41] On April 5, the miscellaneous column of the *Capital Journal* contained this squib: "Walt Pugh, the architect, feels pretty good. So do his friends, over his winning in the city hall contest. It is expected he will put on that silk tie now."

On June 11, 1893, a notice to contractors went out, inviting bids for the erection of a city hall, "according to the plans and specifications on file with W.D. Pugh, architect."[42] On June 23, the committee on the construction of the city hall recommended the acceptance of the low bid of contractors Hutchins & Southwick; however, insofar as that bid ($53,870) exceeded the estimated cost of the building, "sundry changes…that would not impair the strength or appearance of the building in any way" were recommended after

Salem City Hall. *Courtesy of the State Library of Oregon, resource 200400104616.jpg*

a consultation with Pugh, bringing the total of the bid down to $49,617. The *Capital Journal* recorded Pugh's itemized statement for bringing the cost down to that amount. It consisted of fifteen items, most of them cosmetic or interior finishing matters: "Inside walls of tower changed from stone to brick work....Plain wainscotting on ground floor throughout....Second story unfinished...except firemen's quarters....Radiators omitted on second story, except in firemen's bed and sitting rooms." But a few dealt with structural matters: "Truss timbers in roof reduced in size from0 12x16 in. to 10x16.... Reduction of 4 inches in thickness of concrete walls, tower walls excepted."

It is remarkable that the planning and execution of the city hall project coincided almost exactly with the four-year depression set off by the Panic of 1893, which is generally considered to have been the most serious depression in the country's history before the Great Depression of 1929. In the end, the cost of the building came in at $54,675. Pugh's fee of 4 percent of the contract price came to $2,187. This included "services rendered as architect and supervisor of the erection of the city hall."[43]

A moot question: How could the architect, let alone the building committee, have been sure that these reductions would "not impair the strength of the building?" Or, for that matter, how were the original dimensions calculated? The changes were accepted by the contractors and the city's superintendent of construction W.J. Polly, who monitored the construction throughout and was, himself, apparently responsible for some of the changes. Polly pronounced himself fully satisfied with the product: "I think it would be hard to find a better building in all respects."[44]

The article on city hall matters, among other things, in the June 24, 1893 edition of the *Capital Journal* stated in its title, "The New City Hall Will Be Built This Year." This prediction proved overly optimistic. The *Statesman Journal* reported on January 6, 1894, that the basement had been completed, and the bricks were on site. That was apparently enough for the paper to call the building "an Oregon gem." "It is a peculiarly beautiful and wonderfully well adapted structure and is counted without a parallel in its class in the entire Northwest." It also waxed rhapsodic about its creator:

> *It is the creation of Architect W.D. Pugh, of this city, whom no man in Oregon is better qualified to plan such buildings. Mr. Pugh's great forte as an architect is his wonderful faculty of adaptation, and the grouping under one roof of departmental offices in a way that best serves the convenience of the public and the emergencies of official intercommunication.*

"Mr. Pugh," the article concludes, "has a long list of fine buildings behind him to mark his very successful career, and his future prospects are bright with possibilities of numerous other beautiful and model structures that will, in the near future, take palpable shape in this and other neighborhoods."

According to the contract with Hutchins & Southwick, the new city hall was to be completed in 1894. Yet, in February 1895, the *Weekly Oregon Statesman* reported, "Mr. Pugh is still on deck [in the city hall construction] and will personally give his attention to the work. The beautiful structure will stand as an everlasting monument of Mr. Pugh's skill as an architect." These encomia notwithstanding, patience was wearing thin in the city council. In a meeting on February 7, 1895, the city hall committee proposed hiring an assistant superintendent, "as Mr. Pugh had not sufficient time to devote to his work." This proposal was adopted, and a Mr. Henry Harrild was employed as assistant supervisor of construction on an on-call basis.[45]

On February 19, 1895, Pugh was asked to address the city council. The building committee had discovered that the columns in the front of the building that were being built by the contractors did not measure up to the approved plans in possession of the mayor. Pugh explained that he had changed the specifications for the columns after the plans had been submitted to the mayor. After a "long and stormy session," the council resolved to accept the changes, provided that they were present in the drawings on which bids had been submitted.[46]

But the controversy did not end there. At some point before mid-April, Harrild, the assistant supervisor of construction, submitted a report, alleging that the workmanship and materials were "at a variance and fall short of" what was set forth in the building's drawings and specifications.[47] Pugh filed a counterreport, in which, after admitting that certain changes were being made as work progressed, said, "The following, I am confident, will prove to your honorable body, were for the benefit of the building, rather than a detriment, as is the purport of this report." What followed was a detailed account of how the changes were either pre-authorized by the building committee or made in the interest of reducing weight and increasing the strength of structural elements. There was also a detailed discussion of why steel I-beams were used instead of riveted iron box girders. In short, the cost difference was minimal, but the durability and, especially, the carrying capacity of the I-beams was vastly greater, and an authority was quoted with numbers to show the difference. Box girders, moreover, being riveted, were subject to flaws. As for the replacement of round columns with square ones, "The safe carrying capacity of one square column is 229 7–10 tons and one round column is 190 2–10 tons." And there were similar figures regarding floor joists, et cetera. As for Harrild's assertion that an insufficient quantity of cement was used in the mortar for the second story brickwork, Pugh pointed out that it was misdirected, "inasmuch as this particular portion of the building was constructed during the time in which Mr. Harrild was supposed to have been discharging his duty as assistant superintendent."[48] Pugh finished by saying, "In conclusion, if the future work on the city hall building compares with that of the past, it will be a first class piece of work in every particular and equal in every respect to that specified. In this matter, I do not fear successful contradiction."

The paper editorialized that Pugh's explanation of changes appeared to be completely justified and had cost no more, "a feature which redounds to the credit of the architect, whose pride and reputation are equally involved in the successful and acceptable termination of this splendid work."[49] And this was, apparently, the conclusion of the building committee as well. It seems that no further questioning of Pugh's work arose in city council meetings, despite the fact that another two years passed before the construction of the building was complete and it was occupied by city offices. During this time, as noted, some significant, mostly cost-cutting, changes were introduced into plans, including taking some twenty feet off the height of the tower.[50]

This "Oregon gem," with a style that was, at the time of construction, called "classical" and later as "high Victorian Gothic with Romanesque features," became, along with the capitol building, a signature landmark of Salem for many years. It was torn down in 1972, not for any structural failure, but due to overcrowding that came with expansion of the city government, changed building codes and changing fashion. Many Salemites then considered it ugly. Efforts, notably by the Marion County Historical Society, were made to save it—or at least the tower—after a new city hall and civic center were built to the south, but they were unsuccessful. No buyer-occupants could be found for the building, and the revenue from sale of the property had been factored into the construction budget for the new civic center.

This dalliance on some of the details of the city hall project's fulfillment sheds light on the architect's involvement in the construction process when assigned "supervision of construction." The building committee called on the carpet not the contractors who had won the bid for construction but the supervising architect, who, in this case, at least, was conversant with all the details of construction from choice of materials and weight capacity of beams to questions of cost. At the same time, the unusual step taken by the building committee to hire an "assistant supervisor of construction" (albeit on an as-needed basis for four dollars per day) shows that, by early 1895, city officials were growing impatient with the pace of construction and appeared to have concluded that this was due, in part, to Pugh's inability to devote sufficient time to the project.[51] That they should have so concluded can be easily understood by a look at the timeline lists of Pugh's projects as architect or contractor. All of these projects were publicized in the local press at the time.

OTHER MAJOR PROJECTS BEFORE 1900

From the beginning of his architectural career, Pugh was busy with much more than the design of state and local government buildings—he designed schools, of course, but also retail establishments, banks, industrial buildings, buildings for fraternal organizations, opera houses, a hotel, rental houses and private residences. One of the earliest and most imposing of this last category was the so-called Shelton-McMurphey-Johnson house in

"South Elevation," Shelton McMurphey Johnson house, Eugene, Oregon. *Architect's drawing by W.D. Pugh, courtesy of Lane County History Museum.*

Eugene—a large Queen Anne–style frame house with "elaborately eclectic, decorative details…in carved and turned wood." A private residence until the 1980s, it is listed in the National Register of Historic Places and is now maintained as a museum.[52]

The construction firm of Roney and Abrams broke ground on the project, initially estimated to cost $8,000, in May 1887. Pugh must have been working on these plans for a time, at least, as he was simultaneously preparing the plans for Benton Hall at the agriculture college in Corvallis. The construction of the house was nearing completion at the end of November 1887, when it burned to the ground in what was apparently an act of arson. (The generally accepted, if vaguely substantiated, story of the arson says that a local workman who was on the job confessed on his deathbed, many years later, to having set the fire out of a grudge against Abrams, one of the contractors.)[53] The house, built again, was ready for occupancy by October 1888.

Built on the slope of Skinner Butte, the house was ordered by Dr. Thomas Winthrop Shelton (1844–1893). He had come to the Willamette Valley

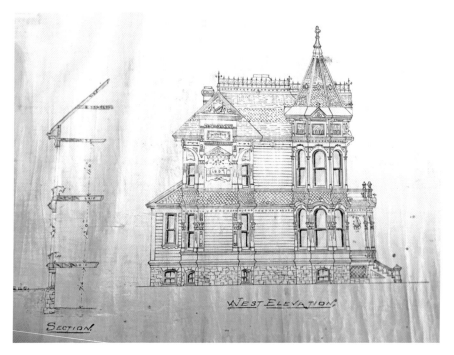

"West Elevation," Shelton McMurphey Johnson house, Eugene, Oregon. *Architect's drawing by W.D. Pugh, courtesy of Lane County History Museum.*

from Missouri as an infant, gotten a medical education in San Francisco and set up a medical practice in Salem. He moved to the Eugene area in 1884, practiced medicine, ran a pharmacy and invested in real estate and other aspects of urban development. The house was built on a hillside of his 320-acre parcel that overlooked the area that became the center of the university town of Eugene. The town eventually became—and long remained—the second most populous city in Oregon.[54] Shelton had moved south before Pugh launched his architectural practice in Salem, but he undoubtedly maintained contacts and probably traveled there frequently by rail. He would have heard of the up-and-coming young architect, even if he had not met him before.

The Queen Anne–style house was very much in vogue throughout Oregon, as elsewhere around the country, in the 1880s, and Pugh may have come to this job with significant experience in the genre of architecture. Around the time of Pugh's apprenticeship there, William McCaw's firm designed several Queen Anne–style houses in the Portland area. It is tempting to see Pugh's hand in the working drawing of the Thornton house.[55]

"East Elevation," Shelton McMuphey Johnson house, Eugene, Oregon. *Architect's drawing by W.D. Pugh, courtesy of Lane County History Museum.*

Before the turn of the century, Pugh designed at least fifteen additional houses, beginning in May 1886 with "a fine cottage on Chemeketa between Twelfth and Capitol Streets" for himself and his bride.[56] Like that one, several of Pugh's residential constructions appear to have qualified as cottages, the term often applied, at the time, to relatively modest, single-story, single-family dwellings with an estimated cost of construction of generally $1,000 or less. But most were more costly residences, coming in at $1,500 or more, and at least three—the Gilbert residence at Chemeketa and Liberty Streets, the Thomas Sims "house and basement" on East State Street (Edes addition) and the E.Y. Lansing "two-story, stone foundation house" near Salem—received contractors' bids in the $4,000 range.[57] It appears that none of these nineteenth-century houses, even the more elaborate ones "with modern conveniences," have survived.[58] Not even the digitized photography archives—the Ben Maxwell Collection, Building Oregon, et cetera— yield results, with rare exception.[59] And finally, there are no copies of plans, elevations or other architect's drawings, as there is no personal archive of the architect or records of a city planning commission (the office came into existence much later, in 1926).

The year 1887 had marked the real launch of Pugh's independent career as a Salem architect. In that year, he took on an astonishing number and variety of projects. By mid-year, he had designed or at least begun designing three private houses, including the Shelton-McMurphey home in Eugene and the A.N. Gilbert home in Salem; a new wing for the insane asylum; a "quite commodious" private sanitorium for Dr. Josephi in East Portland (cost estimate $7,000–$10,000); and three two-story business "blocks" in Salem's commercial center.[60] (See appendix A.) And he must have designed the agricultural college building in Corvallis (later known as Benton Hall) in the first half of that year.[61] Salem, Portland, Eugene and Corvallis—how, in 1887, did he get around to his ongoing projects in these towns that are scattered up and down the Willamette Valley?

In the second half of 1887, in addition to progressing with some of the projects he had taken on in the first half, most notably, perhaps, the agricultural college building, "by direction of the county commissioners of Benton county," Pugh also made preliminary drawings for a new courthouse that was to be erected in Corvallis in 1888. "The style of architecture will be ionic, and the building will be of brick and stone…and will cost in the neighborhood of $55,000." In the end, that contract went to Delos Neer.[62]

"A.N. Gilbert Corner," Liberty and Chemeketa Streets, Salem, Oregon (1887). Photograph circa 1889. *Courtesy of the State Library of Oregon.*

Hotel (Gail Hotel), Dallas, Oregon (1888). *Courtesy of the Polk County Historical Society.*

In 1888, Pugh executed plans for several projects at the state penitentiary, including the construction of a new brick building (laundry, blacksmith and carpentry shop), for which $6,000 had been appropriated, amounting by October of that year to $2,700 "for architectural services."[63] In early March 1888, the *Weekly Oregon Statesman* reported that a building contract had been let to Messrs. Riely and Cead for the construction of a new hotel in Dallas. Designed by Architect Pugh, it was to be "a three-storied structure of modern design, with accommodations for 100 guests." (A follow-up story in May reported that the subscription for funding had been successful and work on the foundation was underway; the total cost, including furnishings, was estimated to be around $6,900.)

The same article that reported on Pugh's work on the penitentiary building noted that he was also working on a new two-story brick building for the State Insurance Company at a cost of $7,000. It also said he was working on four identical rental cottages for John Q. Wilson on Center Street, between Commercial and Liberty Streets—all of these projects were mentioned in a single article in the *Statesman Journal* on March 23, 1888. In May, Pugh was receiving bids on a three-story office building for the same insurance company.[64]

Since the demolition of his signature city hall in 1972, it is in commercial real estate that Pugh's work remains as a significant part of Salem's urban landscape. In the "Oregon SP Salem Downtown State Street–Commercial Street Historic District" item in record group 79 of the National Park Service in the National Archives, three of the fourteen extant buildings listed in the National Register of Historic Places were designed by W.D. Pugh, as were two of the ten "properties designated local landmarks" in the same district.[65] All of them went up between 1889 and 1890.

Of these, the most significant Salem buildings are:

- Bush-Breyman Block, 135–141–147 Northeast Commercial Street (1889) (Breyman portion, no. 74001700).
- Bush-Brey Block and annex, 179–189–197 Northeast Commercial street (1889) (no. 81000505).
- Eldridge Block, 240–254 Northeast Commercial Street (1889).
- Chemeketa Lodge, Odd Fellows Hall and annex (the opera house, Grand Theater), 181–195 Northeast High Street (1900) (no. 88000275).

The three "blocks" were, of course, not city blocks but large commercial premises, usually containing two or more stores or other enterprises at street level; although, in the case of these three projects, the first two came close to being city blocks of uninterrupted building until the Bush portion of the first was demolished in 1960, after a fire, and it has not been replaced. The third, across Commercial Street in the next block to the north, was a very large structure with twenty-three bays, of which only the seven bays of the Greenbaum building, centered under the south tower, remain.[66] All three, as originally built, shared the same style and were made of brick with cast-iron façade ornamentations. The texts accompanying the materials filed with the National Register of Historic Places Office variously describe the buildings' style as Queen Anne or Italianate. The Breyman structure has kept its original façade above the street-level floor, as has the surviving south end of the Eldridge Block.[67] Early lithographs and photographs show that the design and details of the Eldridge Block and the Bush-Brey building's façade closely conformed to the same style. The Bush-Brey building's second-floor interior hall has been preserved as it was originally outfitted.

The full Bush-Breyman Block occupied 119 feet along Commercial Street (the surviving Breyman portion measures fifty-three by ninety feet). The Bush-Brey Block measures seventy-two by ninety feet. According to the

Top, left: Bush-Breyman Block (Breyman portion), Salem, Oregon (1889). *By M.O. Stevens, GNU Free Documentation License, Version 1.2.*

Top, right: Bush-Breyman Block (Breyman portion) detail, Salem, Oregon (1889). *Courtesy of the Design Library, University of Oregon Libraries, I.D. pna_09821.InC/1.0/.*

Middle, left: Bush-Brey Block and Annex (1889). *Drawing from a historic lithograph, National Register of Historic Places, database ref. no. 81000505.*

Middle, right: Bush-Brey Block (1889) today. *By M.O. Stevens, Creative Commons 3.0., unported license.*

Bottom, left: The Boyce building at Commercial and Chemeketa Streets, Salem, Oregon, 1940 (Eldridge Block, 1891). *Courtesy of the Salem Public Library Historic Photographs Collections, Ben Maxwell 1406.*

Bottom, right: South Eldridge Block (the remaining portion of the Greeenbaum building, under the south tower). *Photograph by Thomas N. Green Jr., SHINE on Salem, Salem Heritage Network.*

nomination papers for National Register of Historic Places, "at some time… after 1915," on the south end of the Bush-Brey Block (the Brey portion) on Commercial Street, a Pugh-designed extension of three bays, approximately sixteen and a half feet long and with the exact same style and materials, was added.[68] The Eldridge Block originally reached a total frontage of almost two hundred feet.

These buildings occupied a prominent place in the central commercial district of Salem. They were constructed during a commercial building boom in Salem that was launched by the city's connection to the Oregon and California Railroad in 1871, and, more immediately, they were built as part of a fire-prevention initiative, in which a group of Salem capitalists and merchants bought and tore down two city blocks of wooden buildings and replaced them with cast-iron-fronted brick buildings. The Breyman façade is still intact, except for the street-level floor.[69] All of the cast iron was produced in the Salem Ironworks.[70] Cast-iron-fronted buildings were still in fashion in Portland at the time of Pugh's apprenticeship there. They had been common in the commercial district of Portland since the 1850s, and the fashion had been carried directly to Salem with the outstanding example of the Ladd & Bush Bank, constructed in 1869.[71]

The *Statesman Journal* was particularly enthused by the Eldridge project, which it described in some detail:

> *Then comes the main entrance, 13 feet, 4 inches wide, in which will be a stairway and an elevator. The whole structure will be provided with arrangements for electric lights and gas at the pleasure of the occupiers.…The front elevation of the block will be 53 feet, and over the main entrance will be a tower reaching 25 feet higher, or 78 feet from the foundation.…The upper front will be entirely of pressed brick, the first structure of the kind in the city, and the lower front of iron and plate glass.…The drawings are finely executed and speak flatteringly of Mr. Pugh's abilities as an architect.*[72]

Asahel Bush (1824–1913) appears to have been the initiator of the Brey and Breyman projects; he was a member of the group that financed the demolition of fire-prone wooden buildings in the area and their replacement by brick structures. He then joined with other real estate developers, the Breyman brothers, Werner (1829–1916) and Eugene (1834–1903), and Moritz Brey (1815–1894), in the construction of the two blocks. All of them were pioneer immigrants to Oregon. Bush was a native of Massachusetts, and the others had all emigrated from Germany (Hannover and Hesse-Cassel, respectively). The Breyman brothers had only come to the United States in the 1840s or 1850s, and Brey had come as early as 1834. All had moved about western Oregon and engaged in several enterprises before settling in Salem after it was made the territorial capital in 1853. Bush had worked as a printer and had a law degree; he founded the *Weekly Oregon Statesman* newspaper in Oregon City before moving it to Salem, where he eventually sold it and founded a bank.[73] He was also a principal organizer of the Democratic Party in post–Civil War Oregon. The Breymans had established general merchandise stores in several places before setting up shop in Salem. By 1880, they had gotten out of the retail business and become real estate developers and money lenders. Brey settled in Salem in 1852 as a cabinetmaker. By the mid-1880s, he was a well-known capitalist and real estate developer. Both blocks were built as investments by their owners not as locations for their businesses (with the exception of the Breymans' loan company, which had an office among several others on the second floor of their building).[74] The Breymans had already built a block directly across the street as early as 1874.

Pugh's recent senior partner W.F. Boothby appears to have been the principal organizer of the group that built the big Eldridge Block. It is his portion that survives today. The other principal partner was probably F.E. Eldridge (1827–1890), who owned the opposite, wraparound end of the block that bore his name.[75] He had come to Oregon from Pennsylvania as early as 1849 and had gained wealth in the milling and lumber businesses, among others; then he went into real estate investments. The block was apparently named in his honor after his death.

The final building in the Salem downtown district designed by W.D. Pugh (bearing in mind that the Pugh-designed city hall was demolished before the creation of Salem's Historic District) and listed in the National Register of Historic Places was the uninspiringly named Chemeketa Lodge No. 1 Odd Fellows building (also known as the IOOF Temple and Grand Theatre), built in 1900. In 1894, Pugh had designed a two-story IOOF building in the nearby village of Hubbard, a two-story wooden structure measuring forty-two by fifty-four feet.[76] The much grander Odd Fellows Temple and Opera House was a three-story building designed for commercial use; the Grand Theatre occupied the first floor; offices occupied the second; and the third was devoted to lodge offices. A one-story annex was added on the west side by the same architect in the same year.[77] The construction of 1900 was made of stone and brick, with a cement facing on the upper floors. Its original style was described as "a restrained, late reflection of Richardsonian Romanesque"; such "reflection," it seems, was in the rounded windows and entrance arches. The original frame tower on top of the building (practically a trademark feature of Pugh buildings) was removed after it was damaged in an extra-heavy snowstorm in February 1937.[78] The third-story lodge hall, alone, has preserved something of its original appearance and is fully intact; the theater is spatially intact.

In 1892, Pugh designed a new brick building next to the 1874 Ladd & Bush Bank on South Commercial Street for Asahel Bush and a new fifty-by-one-hundred-foot building to house the electric light and power station of Thomas Holman. But soon after construction began on the station, Holman sold his operation to a large Portland syndicate that intended to install a much larger operation on the premises, requiring an even larger building. The role of architect Pugh—if any—in the changes that followed is unclear.[79]

The brick building boom that got underway in Salem in the late 1880s strained the capacity of local brickyards. More than one project was said to have been waiting on bricks to get underway. Reporting on new developments in brick production, including the buyout and expansion of the old Collins Brickyard by the Burton brothers and the gearing up

IOOF building (Chemeketa Lodge No. 1) (1900). *Courtesy of the State Library of Oregon.*

Above: Grand Theater, Salem, Oregon (originally Chemeketa Lodge No. 1, Odd Fellows). *Photograph by Joe Mabel, Creative Commons attribution 4.0, international license.*

Right: Chemeketa Lodge No. 1, interior detail. *Courtesy of the Design Library University of Oregon Libraries, www/oregon/gov/OPRD/HCD/SHPO.*

of production in the brickyards of the state prison, the *Capital Journal* noted, "It is well known what a hindrance a lack of building material has been to the growth of the city as an instance of these delays caused by lack of brick."[80] The situation persisted: "The brickyards about Salem cannot supply brick fast enough," intoned an article from June 1891. The article further noted that three new lumberyards had been established so far that year.[81]

It was in the same busy year of 1889 that Pugh first undertook the design of an industrial building, properly speaking. "Bids will be received at the office of the Thos. Kay Woolen Mill Co. for the construction of a Woolen Mill building, 110 feet long by 55 feet wide and three stories high. Plans and specifications can be seen at the office of Walter Pugh. Bids will be opened at 2:00 p.m. August 5th."[82] The contract was awarded to F.B. Southwick, who had a low bid of $8,442, on August 15, 1889.[83] This marked the beginning of Pugh's association with Thomas L. Kay (1837–1900) that culminated in the construction of the great brick mill that still stands at the Willamette Heritage Center (listed in the National Register of Historic Places), next to the Willamette University campus in Salem.

The Thomas Kay Company had been founded in 1889 by Kay and two partners. If the *Statesman* story of the time is accurate, it was formed in response to the initiative of a committee of Salem businessmen who were keen on reviving Salem's woolen mill, which had been a leader among Oregon mills until it had burned down in 1876. In this respect, the enterprise appears to have been of a piece with the contemporaneous development of Salem's commercial center.

Kay, "the moving spirit of the enterprise," was a Yorkshireman with a biography of Dickensian proportions.[84] He had gone to work in a woolen factory's spinning department at the age of ten; promoted through various jobs to the trade of weaver, he had immigrated to New York in 1857.[85] He worked in the wool trade on the East Coast before being recruited in 1863 to work as a weave room foreman in a mill in Brownsville, Oregon. By 1875, he was a part owner of Brownsville Woolen Mill, having moved about to work in several mills around the valley, including the Salem predecessor.[86] In 1888, with forty years of experience in the textile business and a considerable reputation, he moved to Salem, where he successfully recruited support and a subscription of funding ($20,000) for his new corporation, which was formed on July 16, 1889. Pugh's plans for the first Thomas Kay Mill must have been in preparation prior to the incorporation, as the mill was already in operation by early 1890.

The first Thomas Kay Woolen Mill, Salem, Oregon (1889). Thomas Kay is standing third from the right. *Courtesy of the Oregon Historical Society Research Library, ba 015883, 59803.*

This first mill building, "considered the most sturdily constructed and modern mill on the coast at the time of its completion" was, like other mills of the region at that time, a frame building.[87] It burned down in November 1895, as had several other frame mills in the Willamette Valley, including the predecessor in Salem that it was designed to replace (the Willamette Woolen Manufacturing Company had burned down on the night of May 2, 1876).[88] The Eagle Woolen Mill Company of Brownsville, where Kay had been recruited to head the weaving department, also burned down in 1864, not long after his arrival there. Among the businessmen who supported the venture were those who had recently invested in replacing entire blocks of wooden buildings in the town's commercial center with brick. Whether a frame structure was chosen for the new Salem mill out of a consideration of cost or the shortage of brick—itself due, of course, to a heightened concern about fire danger among Salem businessmen—is not clear. In any event, the mill was to be made of brick the next time around.

With a number of orders on the books (the mill ran on a to-order basis) and community backing (seventy-one subscriptions were bought for a total of $25,300), the mill was immediately refinanced, and ground was broken for the new brick main building of the mill perhaps as early as late December 1895.[89] The bill came to $85,000. The footprint and even the appearance of the new mill was very close to that of the old one: 58 by 150 feet, two and a half stories and a 9-foot-tall basement (in later years, it was significantly expanded). However, the new mill was designed for fire prevention, principally by the choice of brick rather than frame, and was fitted with the most modern equipment: a hydraulic elevator, a dynamo for electric lighting, pumps for firefighting and, of course, the wool-processing machines proper. This machinery, including looms, carding machines and the dynamo, all ran off a single central drive shaft that ran through the length of the building. It was powered by a millrace on Mill Creek with diverted water from the North Santiam River. Several adjacent frame buildings were completed by April 1896.[90]

Thos. Kay Woolen Mill (1896). *Courtesy of the State Library of Oregon.*

The time constraints on Pugh must have been great, especially considering that he was simultaneously engaged in supervising the construction of the new city hall (see previous section on city halls). In the second half of 1895, other new commitments were limited to designing a few private residences (see appendix A). Kay hired Pugh to pattern the plans after the woolen mill in Waterloo, Linn County, which he had bought two years earlier. At least twice between late August 1895 and the end of the year, Pugh visited Waterloo. (The frame building of the Waterloo mill burned down in 1898, after completion of the brick Salem mill.) On December 6, 1895, the *Statesman Journal* reported that Kay had made arrangements to leave for California to visit some of the factories there "in view of building along similar lines," and it reported that he had "engaged the services of architect W.D. Pugh to accompany him on his trip to assist in calculating the dimensions of the structures which meet with favor." A mill in Oakland was named specifically.[91]

The result was the largest woolen mill in the state for some time and longest-lived operation of its type in Salem. The exterior of the main mill building was designed by Pugh within the constraints of its function, which, among other things, mandated long, cadenced rows of windows, and it was given a certain elegance with curved white stone architraves above its windows and sills of the same material. Judging from surviving photographs, other mills of the period generally had the appearance of elongated sheds or dairy barns.

The Kay family soon bought up enough shares to establish family control of the company; it remained that way until the mill closed down for good in the 1960s. In 1909, Kay's son-in-law and Salem partner, C.P. Bishop, and his sons acquired an idle mill in Pendleton, Oregon, and with the aid of the same kind of bond issue solicited by Kay in Salem, they built an up-to-date plant that laid the foundation of the Pendleton Woolen Mills brand.

CHURCHES

It appears that Pugh designed only two churches in the course of his professional career. The first of these was accomplished fairly early and has survived—with significant restoration—in excellent condition; it has been placed in the National Register of Historic Places (no. 79002111). This church, United Presbyterian Church, or "Whitespires," was built in Albany in the spring of 1891. It has been called an imposing example of

"Whitespires" United Presbyterian Church, Albany, Oregon (1891). *Photograph by M.O. Stevens, www.creativecommons.org/licenses/by/3.0/deed.en/.*

"carpenter Gothic," a rendering of the Gothic church style in wood. The other church designed by Pugh was the First Congregational Church at the corner of Liberty and Center Streets, which was built in 1904. The building was to be about thirty by sixty feet. On May 5, 1904, the papers announced that sealed bids were being accepted in the office of Pugh & Carey, architects, Salem.[92]

BANKS

Walter Pugh designed five banks over the course of his career: the Independence National Bank in Independence, Polk County, near Salem (1891); the Douglas County Bank (Booth Bank) in Roseburg (1902); the Benton County State Bank (Johnson Bank) in Corvallis (1906); the United States National Bank of Salem (1909); and the Redmond Bank in Redmond, Deschutes County (1919). Of the four, two—the Independence National Bank and the Benton County State Bank—are in the National Register of Historic Places, and they both retain most of the original form and design of their elevations.[93]

The nomination form for inclusion in the National Register of Historic Places describes the Independence National Bank as "a fine example of commercial architecture in the high Victorian Italianate style.…It is in excellent condition and retains integrity of form, scale, and design of its two street elevations. The building has been in continual use as a banking institution since its construction." It was entered in the National Register of Historic Places on November 6, 1986. It is still in operation as of this writing.

Pugh's second bank was the Roseburg National Bank, also known as the Booth bank, which was built in 1902 for a group of owners of big timber holdings in Douglas and Coos Counties, led by R.A. Booth of Eugene. At the time, Booth was an Oregon state senator. His brother J.H. Booth became the president and owner of the bank for many years. For this project—and this project only—Pugh teamed with "architect" F.E. Alley of Roseburg.

> *Architects W.D. Pugh of Salem and F.E. Alley of Roseburg spent Saturday in Eugene in consultation with Hon. R.A. Booth concerning the proposed Douglas County bank at Roseburg. The plans, as submitted by Messrs. Pugh and Alley, were approved by the directors and call for a two-story building of pressed brick construction with all modern conveniences and improvements. The estimated cost is $15,000, and the building, when completed, will be a substantial improvement to Roseburg.*[94]

The building still stands solidly on the corner of Oak and Jackson Streets in downtown Roseburg, having long since ceased its operations as a bank and with considerable changes, both inside and out, including the removal of the characteristic corner entrance and vestibule. The name of the last bank to occupy the premises is preserved on the stone band beneath the cornice on Oak Street.

Independence National Bank (1891). *Photograph by 46percent, www.creativecommons.org/ publicdomain/ero/1.0/.*

The former Douglas County Bank (1902). *Photograph by Joe Mabel, www.creativecommons.org/ licenses/by-sa/4.0/deed/en.*

Oregon State Soldiers Home, Roseburg, Oregon. *Courtesy of the California Historical Society Collection at the University of Southern California.*

The selection of Salem architect Pugh to design the Booth bank in Roseburg is not surprising. He must have been well known in Eugene through his work on the Shelton house and McClure Hall projects. Around the same time, in 1902, he was negotiating for the design of an opera house complex there.[95] Moreover, he had been in Roseburg the previous year, 1901, negotiating successfully for the design of a new barracks building and a hospital addition at the Oregon State Soldiers' Home nearby.[96] His association with Frank Alley, who is elsewhere identified as a "Roseburg land attorney," is less obvious.

In 1905, a federal grand jury that was investigating Oregon land fraud cases brought indictments against both Booth brothers and other officials of the Booth-Kelly Lumber Company (two of them Booth relatives), along with "Frank E. Alley, abstracter [*sic*] of Roseburg," on charges of conspiring to "defraud the United States government out of public lands."[97] In the end, all were acquitted of the conspiracy charges. R.A. Booth went on to be elected to the U.S. Senate, and he became a benefactor of both the University of Oregon and Willamette University. H.J., for many years, presided over the bank he owned. Perhaps Alley was signed on to have the authority, as supervisor of construction, to look after the family's interest during construction.

Two of the three remaining bank projects on Pugh's list were undertaken later, in 1906 and 1909, during the most significant partnership of his architectural career with Fred A. Legg, and they will be considered in the next chapter. The third and last bank he designed much later, in 1919, in a period of his life that is less well known and, likewise, merits separate consideration.

W.D. PUGH

ITINERANT CONTRACTOR AND FAMILY MAN

Contractor

Even before Pugh's successful completion of the big city hall project (for which he was engaged as supervisor of construction), he had taken up contracting. It seems to have gotten off to a somewhat rocky start.

In May 1897, W.D. Pugh and his new partner for construction projects Charles (Chas) A. Gray had undertaken some significant work on the interior of the old Marion County Courthouse. The work, described in considerable detail in the local press, was designed to rationalize the space of several departments, render the county clerk's records more secure and deal with the settling of the building's foundation, among other things. It seems likely that the idea of rearranging the labyrinthine interior of the courthouse came from the fulsome praise in the local press of Pugh's organization of the new city hall's interior.

Charles Gray (1863–1911) was the same age as Pugh. Brought to Oregon from Iowa at the age of two by his parents, he had grown up in Salem and, like Pugh, attended Willamette. Before going into contracting and partnering with the architect in the late 1890s, Gray was well known in Salem as the coproprietor, along with his two brothers, of a thriving hardware business. He apparently also owned considerable property in the area, judging from the recordings of real estate transactions in the local press.[98]

The courthouse improvements were accomplished rapidly—in the space of just a few weeks—so as to be finished before the opening of the June term of the circuit court. The bill came to almost $2,500. The paint was hardly dry before a hue and cry were raised in the local press—namely, the *Statesman Journal.* On June 19, 1897, the *Statesman Journal* ran this headline: "WHO IS RESPONSIBLE FOR THE JOBBERY DONE IN THE COURTHOUSE? THE MATTER NEEDS INVESTIGATING." The gist of the accusation of "jobbery" was that County Judge Terrell and County Clerk Ehlen had awarded a contract for improvements to the interior of the courthouse without soliciting competitive bids or public comment, and that the bill had been padded in various ways.

The matter was turned over to the grand jury then in session for investigation into the charges of corruption against the court, or more specifically Judge Terrell; a stop-payment order was placed on the contractors' statements, and grand jury subpoenas were issued to "the architects and contractors" Pugh and Gray, to various workmen on the job, County Clerk Ehlen and several other county officials. When the grand jury failed to deliver any indictments, apparently to the accompaniment of innuendos circulating among the public that Judge Terrell had packed the grand jury, a citizen, G.W. Hunsaker of Jefferson, exercised by reports of the waste of the people's taxes on nonessential improvements to the courthouse in such straitened times, an expenditure that would "greatly increase plaintiff's burden of taxation to his great and irreparable injury," brought suit against County Treasurer Brown to compel him to withhold payment to Pugh & Gray until they could be brought to court and the matters of the work performed and the letting of the contract "be fully and fairly investigated."[99]

In November, Judge Terrell and his fellow county commissioners proposed to district attorney S.L. Hayden that the county itself be added to the "parties defendant" in order to clarify the situation.

Hayden rejected this proposal: There was no suit pending in circuit court; therefore: "this is nothing more nor less than a private suit between Hunsaker and Brown."[100] The case dragged on to year's end and beyond. At the end of December, Circuit Court Judge Hewitt ruled that the original payment drafts to Pugh & Gray be declared forever "null and old [*sic*]." But as it turned out, that action by the county court was only preliminary to new, slightly reduced, "warrants" being issued upon surrender of the old ones.[101] In the end, the county administration got its improvements and the contractors collected their money, or most of it (the difference amounted to about $350). The maneuverings that led to this reduction did not make

McClure Hall, University of Oregon, Eugene, Oregon (1899). *Courtesy of the State Library of Oregon.*

the newspapers. And no apparent damage was done to Pugh's excellent reputation in the capital press.

A quite different milestone of Pugh's early contracting career was the building of the University of Oregon's science hall, later known as McLure Hall, which contract he and his partner for building projects, Chas. A. Gray, won in mid-1899. The building was designed by Rolph H. Miller, a Portland architect. It was completed by the end of February 1900, to everyone's satisfaction, despite a time overrun due to bad weather.[102] Remarkably, the *Salem Statesman Journal* reported a few days later that "yesterday at the university, Contractor W.D. Pugh of the new Science Hall was presented with a fine diamond ring as a slight token of esteem from the workmen who have been employed on the building, says the *Eugene Register* of Saturday."[103] Until it was demolished in 1953, this was the one and only building on the University of Oregon campus associated with his name.[104]

In fact, Pugh was engaged in contracting jobs even before the woolen mill and city hall buildings were completed. (Pugh, it will be remembered, was also supervising construction of the city hall).

First and foremost, he, usually with partner Gray, took on a number of building projects for the Bureau of Indian Affairs, Department of the Interior—namely, schools and related facilities on reservations, as well as schools and entire installations at several off-reservation locations for children of Native American tribes, principally Phoenix, Arizona, and Chemawa, near Salem. Chemawa was the second, and second-largest, boarding school for Native American children to be established in the United States, after the Carlisle Indian School in Pennsylvania. Its first location, dating from 1880, was Forest Grove; in 1885, it was moved to a location adjacent to Keizer, the location of the Pugh and Clagget donation claims.

In 1891, a federal law was passed making education of Native American children mandatory for the first time. It was the resulting rapid expansion of federally funded schools and school-related facilities that Pugh connected with, for the first time apparently, at the Warm Springs Indian Agency in Eastern Oregon. In late November 1896, a Salem paper reported, "Architect W.D. Pugh returned Saturday evening from Warm Springs Indian Agency of Eastern Oregon where he has been supervising the erection of government buildings."[105] He had been there, perhaps not uninterruptedly, since the beginning of September.[106] The following summer, "Chas. Gray and W.D. Pugh, the contractors" left for Warm Springs to begin installation of an elaborate water and sewer system for the government. "They take with them twenty Salem people to work on the contract in skilled and unskilled labor."[107]

Most likely, the successful completion of the Warm Springs jobs then led to a whole series of school contracts for the Bureau of Indian Affairs over the next six-plus years.

Between times, Pugh competed for designing a new courthouse in Eugene. The competition was won by architect Delos Neer, who also designed the Benton County Courthouse in Corvallis. Undaunted, in early 1898, Pugh and Gray traveled to Eugene to bid as contractors for its construction. The low bid went to L.N. Roney.[108]

By far the most ambitious and unusual project vied for at this stage by contractor Pugh, hard on the heels of the successful architectural projects of the city hall and woolen mill, was the installation of defense gun emplacements for Puget Sound at Morrowstown Point. Pugh went to Seattle to make a bid to the Army Corps of Engineers for one of the several installations being planned. Bidding $90,000 against a Portland and a San Francisco firm, he did not get the contract and returned to Salem at the beginning of July 1897.[109]

On March 17, 1898, shortly after the unsuccessful bid on the new courthouse in Eugene, Pugh left for a "two weeks' business trip to Phoenix and other towns in Arizona."[110] On March 25, the *Statesman Journal* reported

The Warm Springs Indian Agency, with an Indian school in the center. *Courtesy of the Oregon Historical Society.*

Students and teachers standing outside the Indian school building on the Warm Springs Reservation, Jefferson County, Oregon (1896). *Courtesy of the University of Oregon Libraries and Special Collections, Lee Moorhouse photographs.*

that C.A. Gray had received a telegram on March 24 from his partner W.D. Pugh informing him that their firm "had secured the contract for the erection of five new buildings for the United States Indian Training School at Phoenix, the amount of the contract approximating $40,000. The buildings are to be constructed of brick and fitted with all modern conveniences. Salem is pleased in having one of its firms so fortunate as to secure this large contract, in the face of competition from every important town on the Pacific coast."[111]

In December, he was reported to be in Arizona again bidding for other contracts to be let in Phoenix and other points in Arizona: a government building at the San Carlos reservation, a dormitory for the Phoenix school, a public school in Phoenix, even the territorial capitol building ($150,000) "and a number of others."[112] In May 1899, Pugh was reported superintending work on the School contract, for several months already, and was expected to return on June 2.[113] On June 19, "W.D. Pugh and his family have just returned from Arizona where he has completed some large contract work."

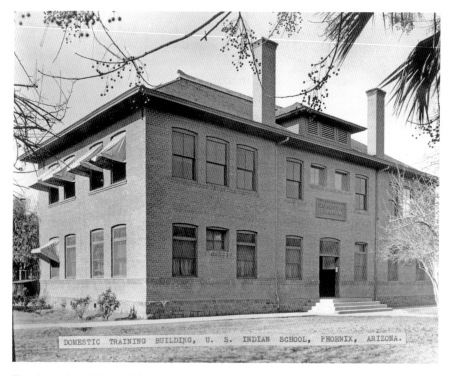

The domestic training building at the Phoenix Indian School, Phoenix, Arizona (circa 1898). *Courtesy of the Arizona State Library, History and Archives Division, Archives and Public Records.*

Classroom building, Phoenix Indian School, Phoenix, Arizona (circa 1898). *Courtesy of the Arizona State Library, History and Archives Division, Archives and Public Records.*

According to the *Phoenix Herald* of June 9, Pugh and family left for a month's visit to Salem. He had just returned from Needles, California "where he has charge of the building of an Indian school dormitory."[114]

The school in question was the Fort Mohave Indian School at the reservation with land in the states of California, Nevada, and, at the time, Arizona Territory. It seems likely that the San Carlos Indian School building at Fort Apache, photographed in the early 1900s by G.E.E. Lindquist, was built by Pugh as well.

By August 1899, Pugh and Gray were back in Oregon, at Eugene, making preparations to begin construction of the science building at the University (McClure Hall).[115] But construction contracts with the federal government for buildings at special schools for Native American children continued into 1901–2, with successful bids, in 1899 and 1900, at Siletz, and in October 1901 for several brick buildings at the Chemawa Indian School at Keizer: a large girls' dormitory ($19,386), an industrial building ($5,040), a steam laundry ($3,494).[116]

Opposite, top: San Carlos Indian School, Arizona (1898–1899, possibly). *Courtesy of Columbia University Libraries, G.E.E. Lindquist Papers, the Burke Library Archives at Union Theological Seminary, New York.*

Opposite, middle: Siletz Indian School Buildings on "Government Hill," Confederated Tribes of Siletz Indian Reservation, Lincoln County, Oregon (1899–1900). *Courtesy of Confederated Tribes of Siletz Indians of Oregon.*

Opposite, bottom: Industrial building (1901), Chemawa Indian School, Salem, Oregon. *Courtesy of the State Library of Oregon.*

Above: Chemawa girls in front of the dormitory (1901), Chemawa Indian School, Salem, Oregon. *Courtesy of State Library of Oregon.*

The Chemawa projects of 1901–2 were carried out with a new partner for those specific jobs, Fremont Van Patten, a Salem carpenter and contractor, who had been one of the building contractors for the Odd Fellows building. It is not hard to understand why Pugh needed a partner for the new Chemawa undertaking. A week after winning the contract for the Chemawa buildings, Pugh & Van Patten ran an ad in the Salem papers: "Fifty Teams Wanted. Four Dollars Per Day. Chemawa."[117]

It is less than obvious why Chas Gray did not continue in the partnership for the big Chemawa projects of 1901–2. Their partnership seems to have been in place by late 1896, with their work supervising installations of waterworks at Warm Springs and Chemawa. (In December 1896, Gray

The interior of the steam laundry building (1901), Chemawa Indian School, Salem, Oregon. *Courtesy of the State Library of Oregon.*

was reported to be superintending the completion of the waterworks system at Chemawa). And in March, 1899, he was reported to be "supervising architect" on a nearly completed brick assembly hall at Chemawa.[118] Pugh and Gray had then collaborated in the competition for building the courthouse in Eugene in 1897, in an architectural project to replace several commercial buildings in Woodburn after the fire there, and later in the improvements to the courthouse in Salem. Here, in the subpoena to appear before the grand jury, they were formally identified as "partners in business under the firm name and style of Gray & Pugh [*sic*]."[119] Then came the building of McLure Hall at the university in 1899–1900. The final, architectural, projects of the partnership, in 1900, were for a cottage at the corner of Church and Center Streets, another one on the grounds of the State Hospital, and finally for a new wing of the State Penitentiary.[120]

Why the Pugh-Gray collaboration did not remain in place for the major construction projects of 1901–2 at the Chemawa school remains an open question. It was not the end of Gray's contracting career. In 1902, he was independently bidding for a bridge construction job on the Santiam River at Gates (successful), and for supplying 2,500 cubic feet of rock to the Army Corps of Engineers for revetment work on the Willamette River near Independence.[121] Nor was it the end of his connection with Chemawa. In April 1903, the *Oregon Daily Journal* reported on the dedicatory exercises at Chemawa on the formal closing of the cornerstone of Mitchell Hall, the new dormitory for boys: "Depositing letter, papers, mementoes and sealing stone, by Charles A. Gray, contractor, Salem, Or."[122] Now contracting on his own, Gray may have outbid Pugh for this significant Chemawa building.

In 1908, Gray, with partners McLean and Perry, incorporated as Portland-based commercial real estate brokers and he and his wife moved to Portland the following year.[123] In 1911, Charles A. Gray died at the age of forty-seven. His two brothers/former partners were then living in Seattle. "Mr. Gray graduated from Willamette University and engaged in the contracting business, constructing, among other prominent buildings, the Indian school at Chemawa. He numbered among his friends many of the most prominent men in the state and was a close personal friend of Governor West."[124] Mrs. Gray (neé Lillian Richardson) remained socially prominent, serving, for example, as Oregon Building hostess at the Panama-Pacific Exposition at San Francisco in 1915.[125]

Later on, as noted, Pugh would partner with other architects or builders for specific jobs and with two more architects in formal partnerships: P.P. Carey, for less than a year in 1904–5; and Fred A. Legg, with whom he had a more active and involved professional association, from the beginning of 1906 to mid-1909.[126] The numerous products of their partnership will be dealt with in the next chapter.

On all the projects for the Bureau of Indian Affairs of the Department of Interior over the span of more than six years, of which the off-reservation schools of Phoenix and Chemawa were the biggest, Pugh & Gray, then Pugh and Van Patten, operated strictly as building contractors. All plans and specifications were supplied by the bureau.[127] Most of these buildings have disappeared over time and so, apparently, have their original plans and specifications. Old photographs and drawings of some of them do exist, and in several cases, it is possible to identify them with reasonable confidence as construction jobs of Pugh & Gray or Pugh & Van Patten. These are listed in appendix A with appropriate notation in order to convey some idea of the scale and magnitude of this aspect of W.D. Pugh's overall contribution to the built landscape.

There is no reason to think that Walter Pugh and his fellow contractors, or for that matter the newspapermen who reported on their Bureau of Indian Affairs projects, were concerned about the program of cultural conversion and assimilation that would be pursued within the walls they built or that they were even aware of it as such.

Traveling Man

It is impossible to observe our protagonist exercising his profession in the 1880s and 1890s, moving about a large area of the Pacific Northwest, even into the Southwest, with what appears to have been remarkable speed and facility, without examining how this was possible in the late nineteenth century.

To a very large extent, he traveled by rail. With the completion of the transcontinental lines, Oregon's population entered a period of rapid growth. Between 1870 and 1900, the state's population grew from 90,000 to 413,000. Over the same period, an explosion of railroad building, from regionwide lines to very local ones, seized the Willamette Valley, fueled by promises of local prosperity and access to markets and financed largely by the sale of bonds. Towns, some today mere shadows of their never very populous selves, were linked by rail to each other and to the wider world for a time, and a few remained connected by feeder lines, which were eventually used only for freight, to the transcontinental giants Northern Pacific and Union Pacific Railroads and to the north–south Oregon and California (O&C), later Southern Pacific, Railroad. The O&C line from Portland had reached Eugene, through Salem, by 1871, and it reached Roseburg before the end of 1872. There was passenger service from Salem to Portland with stops in between—a local stop was located in Chemawa—and it went as far south as Roseburg. Only in 1884 did it reach as far south as Ashland, and in 1887, Southern Pacific (SP) took over and opened through service from Portland to California. By 1890, lines connected to the SP in southern California and led to Phoenix, Arizona, and even Needles, California. Getting from Phoenix to Needles apparently required a retreat to the SP mainline, then taking a passage north a short distance to Mojave, California, to reach the Needles–Fort Mohave connection.

The rail connection between Portland and Seattle, with a ferry crossing at Kalama, was established in 1884 (the all-rail route came with construction of the Columbia River Railroad Bridge between Portland and Vancouver, the first bridge of any kind across the lower Columbia River, in 1908).

The O&C/SP ran a line west of the Willamette River, from Portland to Corvallis, in 1879, linking numerous townships. Before World War I, the Oregon Electric Railroad on the east side of the Willamette River linked the Portland–Eugene stretch with a number of towns that were bypassed by the O&C/SP line.

There was easy rail access to Corvallis through Independence. From Independence to Valsetz and Siletz in the coastal range, the Valley & Siletz Railroad could be taken. Another Portland–Corvallis line was run by the Western Oregon Railroad as early as 1880. From Salem, at that time, a passenger could transfer from the main north–south O&C/SP line at Albany and take an Oregon Pacific train daily to Corvallis, or they could even continue westward all the way to Yaquina, a point on Yaquina Bay between Toledo and Newport, where a regular steamer carried passengers to Newport and the ocean beaches. For a time, passengers could travel on a steamship run by the same company all the way to San Francisco.

The Corvallis founders of the line dreamed of "switching poles" with Portland, sending Willamette Valley commerce and passengers southward, through Corvallis, to Yaquina Bay, which was several days (by sea) closer to San Francisco than Portland. Eastward from Corvallis, the aim was to extend the railroad, through Albany, across the Cascade Mountains and eastern Oregon, to meet up with the Union Pacific and thus establish Yaquina Bay and Corvallis as terminals of transcontinental routes. The Western Oregon Railroad reached a point on what is now the Detroit Dam on the North Santiam River. It bypassed Lebanon (a few miles from Waterloo), so the twelve-mile Albany & Lebanon Railroad was built in 1880.[128] Brownsville was reached from the Central Valley by the Oregonian Railway, which linked it to Lebanon and other points to the north and west. Dallas could be reached from Portland on a line from the same company.[129]

The names of towns with buildings that were designed or constructed by Walter Pugh and are mentioned here are only a few of the many that were connected by rail in the pre-automobile history of Oregon. It may be that the sole locations that lacked a rail connection at the time of Pugh's visits for major projects were Warm Springs and Prineville in central Oregon. Having been bypassed by the north–south Oregon Trunk Line, the town of Prineville itself built a trunk line to it but only in 1916. Warm Springs was fifteen miles from Madras on that north–south line to Klamath Falls.

In 1881, the Westside Division of the O&C's daily train from Portland to Corvallis left Portland at 8:00 a.m. and arrived in Corvallis at 3:00 p.m.—if it ran according to schedule. The Oregon electric trains made the run from Portland to Corvallis in two hours and forty minutes, and they could go all the way to Eugene in three hours and sixteen minutes, the same qualification applying.

Many of the short lines of the time, including some of the shortest, published timetables showing fares not only to Portland but to Denver, Chicago, New York and many of the major cities in between.

FAMILY MAN

In 1885, within five months of his return to Salem from his Portland apprenticeship, in "a very pleasant wedding...Mr. Walter D. Pugh and Miss Fannie E. Rhodes, all of this city," were married at the residence of the bride's parents.[130] He was twenty-two, and she was not quite seventeen.[131] Fannie was the daughter of Allan Rhodes (1841–1915), who was born in England to the family of a wool-spinner; he was a fixture in Salem for many years as a taxidermist. He also worked, at various times, as a night watchman at the courthouse, a guard (or custodian) at the insane asylum and other occupations. Fannie's mother, Mary Rhodes (1840–1917), also from England, was active in the Salem Woman's Christian Temperance Union for many years.

The young couple's first child, Inez, was born in March 1886, and in May, the young architect had built for his family "a fine cottage on Chemeketa between Twelfth and Capitol Streets."[132] They had two more children: Allen, born in 1888, and Albert, born in 1891.[133]

Fannie's name turns up occasionally in the Salem papers from those years: a birth notice for her second child, Allen, in 1888 and the fact that "Architect W.D. Pugh and wife came up from Salem on their wheels and are taking in the sights" in Waterloo, where Pugh went several times in the mid-1890s to examine the woolen mill there.[134] Walter took Fannie and the children with him to Phoenix, Arizona, during at least one long stay there, occupying most of the first half of 1899, for work on the Indian school jobs.[135] The *Capital Journal* reported on June 30, 1900, "Mrs. Walter Pugh and children started yesterday over the O.R.&N. lines for a short visit to St Paul and Chicago," probably to visit family on her mother's side.

On September 21, 1901, the *Capital Journal* reported that Walter Pugh went to Portland that day, "where Mrs. Pugh is at St. Vincent's hospital undergoing an operation"; and then, on September 27, it reported that she had died "of abscess of the bowels."[136] Her body was brought to Salem for a funeral and burial in Salem Pioneer Cemetery. On September 28, the *Statesman Journal* ran a longer article about her death "of an abdominal tumor." According to that article, Mrs. Pugh had been suffering from this ailment for about six weeks before taking a serious turn for the worse and being transported to St. Vincent's in Portland, where she underwent an operation and seemed to be recovering. She then took another turn for the worse, lapsed into a semi-conscious state and passed away peacefully at 8:00 p.m. on September 27. Husband and children, her husband's brother Edward and her mother were all in attendance. Her father was in Alaska at the time. The deceased left three children, Inez, age fifteen; Allen, age thirteen; and Albert, age ten.[137]

Shortly after his wife's death, on October 1, 1901, Pugh, partnered with Fremont Van Patten, was awarded the contracts for new buildings at Chemawa Indian School by the Bureau of Indian Affairs. All of the buildings to be completed by June 15, 1902.[138] On January 13, Pugh was back in Portland on business.

At this busy time in his building activities, Walter Pugh succeeded in finding a new wife and took a three-week honeymoon trip by steamer to San Francisco. "On Tuesday, February 25, 1902, at the home of Edward H. Pugh, in Salem, Miss Jessie Hobson was married to Walter D. Pugh, Rev. H.A. Ketchum of the Presbyterian Church performed the wedding ceremony."[139] And on February 26, "Mr. and Mrs. W.D. Pugh departed for Portland on yesterday's afternoon overland, from where they will sail for San Francisco on the steamer *Columbia*. They returned on March 18, 'having completed an extensive wedding tour.'"[140]

Jessie Hobson was born into a pioneer family that had settled in what was to become the hamlet of Sublimity, near Salem. Her grandfather Hadley Hobson had come to the valley over the Oregon Trail and staked a land claim just east of Salem in 1844. Like Walter's father and uncles, he had joined the California gold rush in 1849 and then returned to his claim in Oregon with enough gold to open a general store. His son Lemuel married Sarah Lizette Parker of the pioneer family that was living on an adjacent claim. Jessie, one of their eleven children, was born in 1880.[141]

Jessie and Walter had two children: Katherine, named for her paternal grandmother and born in 1903, and Mildred Irene, born in 1908. Seventeen years younger than her husband, Jessie lived long enough to give cogent interviews to the newspapers in an ultimately unsuccessful civic campaign in 1972 to save the Salem City Hall from destruction. She died in 1983 at the age of 102.[142]

4

BACK TO ARCHITECTURE

1902–1909

On New Year's Day in 1903, the *Statesman Journal's Illustrated Annual 1903* celebrated two local businesses: R.M. Wade, "the oldest firm in the state of Oregon in its line [hardware]," and leading architect W.D. Pugh.

> *W.D. Pugh, the leading architect of Salem was born forty years ago. He received his education in the Salem public schools and Willamette University. Early in life, he demonstrated that he possessed a mechanical brain, and while yet a boy, began his career as an architect. He has planned and superintended the construction of some of the finest buildings in Oregon. His services are sought for from far and near. He has just finished a fine brick block in Roseburg for the Douglas County Bank, which is a credit not only to Mr. Pugh but to the contractors and builders, as well as to the bank people who own it. Mr. Pugh has secured the plans for the Eugene Opera House, which, when completed, will be one of the finest playhouses in Oregon. The contract price for this building will be in the neighborhood of $22,000.*[143]

Eugene, once again, was a site of Pugh's architectural assignments not long after the Roseburg bank job, for which he had traveled to Eugene several times for consultation with R.A. Booth. Before the end of 1902, Pugh, who was by then well known in town, and having recently designed the opera house (also known as the IOOF Chemeketa Lodge/Grand Theater) in Salem, was awarded the design for a new opera house in Eugene. On December 16, he was in Eugene to sign the contract to draw the plans and "preside over the construction."[144] The plans were accepted, and bids were solicited for the opera house; "a brick building for theatre and storeroom purposes" was to be constructed on the property next to Day and Henderson's block on Willamette Street (490–636 Willamette Street) on January 30, 1903. The plans could be seen at the offices of W.D. Pugh in Salem or Eugene.[145] The Eugene Theatre, as it was known until 1922, when its new owner changed its name to Heilig Theater, had 760 seats. Despite Eugene's modest population (around four thousand in 1903), the theater's boards were trod by many big-name entertainers and troupes of the period. It gradually evolved into a movie theater, typical for the opera houses of this era, and it exclusively presented movies from 1926 until its demolition in 1973.[146]

From the completion of the Chemawa buildings, roughly mid-1902, to mid-1909, Walter Pugh concentrated on architectural projects (including several "supervision of construction" assignments) almost exclusively. This was, once again, a period of great diversity for Pugh—from private homes to commercial buildings, including the opera house and banks, to the medical college building at Willamette University and state, county and municipal institutions, including schools, additions to the insane asylum (state hospital), buildings for the new Institution for the Feeble-Minded and Epileptic, various additions and improvements to the state fairgrounds, the Marion County exhibit at the centenary Lewis and Clark Exposition in Portland (1905) and even a platform for the upcoming visit of President Roosevelt (1903). Among these, the schools, banks, medical college and feeble-minded home buildings stand out—or stood out at the time. Only the medical college and the two bank buildings have survived.

Meanwhile, back in Salem, Pugh had managed to execute plans for a two-story brick business block for Maurice Klinger on State Street; a two-story building with a basement next to the Klinger Block for August Schreiber, a liquor store proprietor; a one-story school building in School District No. 60; and a new livery stable on the lot next to W.C. Tillson & Co.'s Feed Store (65 by 165 feet and two stories).[147] Finally, in May, bids were being taken in Pugh's office for an extension of a dining hall and "another closed cottage," similar to the one that had been erected the previous summer, at the insane asylum.[148] Numerous "cottages" were built to house physicians and some other employees of the asylum over the years. (Not to be confused with the "Cottage Farm," large house-like structures that were built on a nearby 640-acre parcel that had been purchased with a legislature-apportioned $30,000 in 1889. Combining living, sleeping and dining facilities for as many as eighty patients each, they were meant to provide a more family-like ambience than the asylum buildings proper.) Some of these cottages on the original asylum territory survived to be included in the National Register of Historic Places. But apparently due to the fact that the state hospital complex as a unit was proposed for inclusion in the National Register of Historic Places rather than its individual structures, the design of the cottages as a whole and individually over the years is attributed in the proposal documents to a whole group of architects, including, in addition to W.D. Pugh, such well-known Oregon architects as Pugh's former senior partner W.F. Boothby (1840–1912), Edgar M. Lazarus (1868–1939), William C. Knighton (1864–1938), Pietro Belluschi (1899–1994) and several others.

By the time of the Eugene Theatre project, if not earlier, Pugh maintained an office in Eugene. He submitted plans for a new Eugene High School at the beginning of April 1903. On April 13, his plans for "a fine stone and brick structure, which will cost in the neighborhood of $25,000" were adopted by the Eugene district school board.[149] On June 4, the contract was awarded to Welch & Mourer, a Salem firm, for the construction of the new school building at the corner of Willamette and Eleventh Streets on a bid of $24,259, "including ventilation and heating apparatus….Construction to begin as soon as school is out…every effort will be made to have the building ready for the opening of the school term next fall." It would be "the finest high school building in the Willamette Valley."[150] This massive, three-story, dormered attic, redbrick building with a corner tower and a first floor with stone facing appears to be a good example of the second renaissance revival that was popular for public buildings around the turn of the century. It is hard to believe that its construction could have been completed in three months, and perhaps it was not; in any case, its formal dedication took place on January 22, 1904. In the end, the cost came in at $32,000.[151] Around 1915, the high school building became Eugene's city hall, and it remained that way until 1962, when a new city hall building was constructed. The former high school building was demolished shortly thereafter.

For nearly half a century, Salem, Corvallis and Eugene had functioning city halls designed by W.D. Pugh.

While simultaneously preparing the plans for the new school in Eugene, Pugh was engaged to design some additions and alterations to a dormitory at the University of Oregon in Eugene and the extension of a dining hall and yet another "closed cottage" at the insane asylum in Salem.[152]

Almost exactly one year after dedication of the Eugene High School, Pugh's plans for a new $50,000 high school in Salem were approved by

Eugene High School (1903). *Courtesy of the State Library of Oregon.*

the Salem School Board. For eighteen months, between the acceptance of the plans for the Eugene High School and the acceptance of those for the Salem high school, Pugh was in a partnership with P.P. Carey. The *Statesman Journal* reported the new association, remarking that the firm had considerable work on hand, "which is not surprising, considering their known ability and the amount of prospective improvements in Salem."[153] In March, the *Capital Journal* carried an article confirming the anticipation of a building boom in Salem, and it reported that Portland architect W.C. Knighton had opened an office in town, "while the other architect operating here, W.D. Pugh, is also kept busy with work."[154]

But then, on December 30, 1904, the Salem papers carried a message: "NOTICE OF DISSOLUTION. The firm of Pugh & Carey, Architects, has this day, by mutual consent, dissolved. Mr. Carey retiring. Mr. Pugh will continue the business, occupying the same offices at 116 State Street, Salem, Oregon. Signed by both, dated Dec. 7, 1904."[155]

It appears that Pugh had taken on Carey as a draftsman during this busy time in his career. Excerpts from a letter Carey wrote to a Salem friend from his native England (near Turnbridge Wells, Kent) in 1938 were published in a Salem newspaper with this introduction: "While here, in the employ of other architects, he drafted the plans for the old Salem high school, Oregon School for the Deaf, and other schools and state buildings."[156] Immediately before joining up with Pugh, Carey was employed as an attendant in the male wards of the insane asylum, but it seems that he had been associated with Pugh earlier, during the Pugh & Gray contracting period, some time before spring 1899.[157] On April 18, 1899, the *Capital Journal* reported, "P.P. Carey, of Philomath, is in the city. Mr. Carey was formerly associated with Pugh & Gray as an architect."[158] And a few days later, in the same paper, it was reported: "P.P. Carey, late of Kansas City and at one time located here, has returned to Salem and opened an architect's office in the Holman Block."[159] And for several months, beginning in May 1899, Carey ran an advertisement in the Salem papers: "P.P. CAREY, architect. No. 9 Holman Block, Salem. Mapping, blue printing, patent office drawings, mechanical drawings." In fact, he had returned to Salem as early as July 1897, as noted in the "personals" column of the *Statesman Journal*: "P.P. Carey, a draftsman and photoengraver, is again in Salem. He resided here four years ago."[160]

Considering the number of projects Pugh was working on at the same time, it seems entirely possible that Carey had a hand in drafting the plans for the Salem high school. Perhaps his services as a draftsman were in such demand that Pugh chose to formalize their relationship. In any case, Pugh alone is generally identified as the author of the plans for those and other projects of that period.

It is not known when Carey returned to England. In 1910, he and his wife purchased 137.7 acres near Salem (for $2,500). He may have been working with Fred A. Legg for some time between the end of the Pugh & Legg partnership and Legg's closing of his Portland office in 1915 or 1916; at least we can find a 1911 "Notice to Contractors and Builders" that says the plans and specs for the construction of a two-room schoolhouse in Marion County School District 3 could be examined "either at Legg & Carey's office or at the clerk's residence."[161] And Carey was still listed on the published school tax rolls in 1929.[162] Perhaps it was the onset of the Great Depression that year that provoked his return to his homeland. The plans for the new Salem high school may have been the last job of his collaboration with Pugh, as those plans were approved on January 24, 1905.[163]

SALEM TO HAVE A NEW HIGH SCHOOL, TO COST ABOUT $50,000

The school board unanimously accepted the building proposed by Mr. Pugh: a three-story-plus-basement building of either pressed or cream buff brick…171 feet long by 80 feet wide, with cement basement and attic. There will be sixteen rooms, including a large assembly room on the second floor.… [The] *plans specify three entrances, each to be connected with the second floor of the building by a large stairway. The sixteen rooms would accommodate forty-eight pupils each. This would allow fifteen square feet of space and 200 cubic feet of air to each scholar. The structure would be splendidly equipped with the latest lavatories and would also include two large gymnasium rooms, one for the girl pupils.…The members, as a body, unanimously favor the use of pressed or cream buff brick…as it would entail an additional expense of only $2,200. Several of the members of the school board openly expressed their disfavor of the use of plain brick. They said they would rather have no high school at all than to have one built of old common brick, as it would present a very commonplace appearance.… About 350 pupils will be ready to enter the high school course of instruction by next fall.* [In fact, occupancy was delayed until January 2, 1906].…*Salem will have a high school building by the coming fall term that will compare favorably with any similar educational structure in this or adjoining states.*[164]

A case in point was the Pugh-designed Eugene High School, which was completed a year earlier by the same Salem contractors, Welch & Mourer. Their styles were essentially the same, but the Salem school was considerably larger, occupying a full half block, but it had no tower and was not made of red brick (it was made of pressed brick). A comparison of surviving color photographs of the two buildings confirms the good taste of the several Salem school board members: a building of that size in red brick would have appeared grotesque. The construction of the Salem high school, on the block bordered by Marion, High, Center and Church Streets, Northeast, began in April 1905. Its formal dedication took place on January 1, 1906. It ended up costing $60,000.[165] The *Statesman Journal* devoted an entire page to eulogy-like descriptions of the new school: "ONE OF THE FINEST SCHOOL BUILDINGS ON THE COAST, CREDIT TO ANY CITY. School to Be Opened in this Building this Morning, and It will Be Pointed Out as One of the Structures Giving Standing and Character to Our City." And further: "It is a beautiful structure externally, with its pressed brick walls and modern style of attractive architecture, and is as nearly perfect in the arrangement and furnishings of the interior as the skill of the human brain and hand can make such a building."[166] The article goes on to describe, at some length, such novel features as forced-air heating and ventilation (installed by the Portland firm of W.G. McPherson); wood-fiber plastered walls in the classrooms; seating arranged so that light comes from the left of the pupils, considered the best arrangement (for right-handed pupils); a fine auditorium and assembly room on the second floor, "with a large, roomy stage and excellent acoustics." The article continues: "[T]he beauty of the building, its completeness of arrangement and its splendid finish in every respect, will stand as a monument to the credit of Salem's public spirit, to the intelligence of its board of directors and to the architectural ability and taste of Mr. W.D. Pugh, architect and superintendent."

The article then turns to the authors of this achievement: the aforementioned McPherson company, the contractors and the architect.

> *The structure will stand as a monument to his taste and skill for a thousand years. Mr. Pugh has been furnishing plans for and superintending the construction of buildings here and hereabouts for twenty-five years. Practically all the best buildings recently erected here have been according to his plans and specifications, and under his supervision. They include, among many others, the Salem City Hall, Odd Fellows' Temple, First Congregational church, medical college, and many state buildings.*[167]

The article then turned to the contractors, Welch & Mourer, and included a sizeable block of text accompanied by photographic portraits, from which we learn that they were the contractors for several previous buildings designed by W.D. Pugh, including the Klinger and Schreiber Block, on State Street near High Street; the First Congregational Church; and, of course, Eugene High School.

Both W.M. Welch and G.C. Mourer, like Pugh, were men in their forties with youthful experience in the building trades. Welch was previously a carpenter, and Mourer was a stone- and brickmason. From these experiences, they apparently made successful entrepreneurial leaps into a contracting partnership in a time of rapid population growth and abundant construction opportunities in Oregon.

The new high school did not stand for a thousand years, of course. The 1906 building that had been designed for an estimated 350 pupils was replaced in 1937 by one designed for 2,000. The bill for this new school came

Salem High School (1905). *Courtesy of the University of Oregon Libraries, Special Collections and University Archives.*

in at more than ten times the cost of the Pugh-designed school (unadjusted). Starting in 1937, the old high school building served as the school district administration building. It was demolished in 1954 to make way for the new Meier & Frank Department Store.

That such large buildings could be constructed in such a short amount of time, whether it was three or even nine months, at the beginning of the twentieth century seems quite remarkable—even considering that a variety of inspections that are required today, including inspections for biohazards, wheelchair access, environmental impact, et cetera, were absent at the time.

Plans for downtown Salem blocks continued apace: a new building for E.S. Lamport at 289 Commercial Street in early 1904, "a fine two-story brick building" on the corner of Liberty and State Streets for the heirs of Louis Verani, a two-story block for D.F. Wagner next to Steusloff Bros. (387 Court Street) in the spring of 1905.[168] Plans for the Congregational church on the corner of Liberty and Center Streets had been readied for bids by May 1904.

Salem Congregational Church (1904). *Courtesy of the Salem Public Library Historic Photograph Collections, Ben Maxwell 0245.*

In the spring of 1905, Pugh was involved in design projects with the state fair board and the Marion County exhibit for the 1905 centenary Lewis and Clark Exposition in Portland.

The $15,000 appropriation for fairground improvements mainly involved additions to existing structures: the banquet hall, the pavilion, the grandstand, roofing over ground space between buildings, decomposed granite sidewalks and so on. (The impressive twin-towered, three-arched entrance gate was built later, in 1909, from plans drawn by Fred A. Legg. "No one seems to know when it was torn down.")[169] The total bill for these architectural services came, apparently, to $627. At least that was the amount paid "for architect's services in the year's improvement at the fairgrounds," as reported in the press.[170]

The Marion County "booth" in the Oregon building of the Lewis and Clark Exposition in Portland was taken quite seriously by the City of Salem and Marion County authorities. Pugh was hired to design the booth, and the Brown and Lehman Sash and Door Factory was hired to build it. The booth was to present Marion County products that were to compete for jury-awarded medals.

> [The booth], *in the nature of a series of artistically designed arches, with an imitation tiled roof…is truly a work of art, as it has been pronounced by all who have seen it.…The arches, that is, their bases, are provided with a double row of panel-like receptacles for the display of fruit, vegetables, etc., in boxes and crates, and is capable of being transformed into a most attractive exhibit. The balance of the booth is composed of fancy panel work made of native Oregon woods, and the central cornice is richly and elaborately decorated with inlaid work of highly polished Oregon hardwoods.*[171]

Unfortunately, the collections of historic Oregon photographs that are available online provide very little images of the structure's details.[172] William Savage, the superintendent of the exhibit, was not wrong in predicting that the Marion County exhibit "will not be left entirely in the shade when the time for judging arrives." The exhibit and its exhibitors received fifty-one gold medals, thirty-five silver medals and twelve honorable mentions. The county ranked first in rank of awards. Of course, the individual awards were for the production of everything from hops and harnesses to jams and jellies, but their presentation was not neglected as a factor in their success.[173]

At the end of its encomium on Pugh the article on the high school opening cited previously goes on to provide this additional information about the firm:

> *Recently, Fred A. Legg has become a partner of Mr. Pugh, and the firm is Pugh & Legg.…This firm is well equipped for furnishing and doing anything that is undertaken by architects in any city. They are enjoying a large business, not confined entirely to this city or section, for their ability is recognized everywhere, and their customers are found all over the Pacific Northwest.*

This new partnership was first announced in the capital press in April 1905 in an article that reported the sale of the Red Corner Drugstore: "Mr. Legg has been in the drug business in Salem for the past sixteen years, and he retires in order to enter the office of W.D. Pugh, the architect, as a partner. Mr. Legg has been studying along this line for a long time.…He will add materially to the reputation of Salem in this line, which is already good."[174] This partnership, which lasted until mid-1909, was the single relatively long-lasting strictly architectural partnership of Pugh's career. During this partnership, a number of projects of considerable significance were undertaken. Three of these—the medical college (presently the art department) on the Willamette University campus, the Johnson Bank in Corvallis and the United States National Bank of Salem—are still standing.

Frederick Arthur Legg (1869–1941), like Pugh, was the son of pioneer parents (of the 1847 migration). He was born in Portland, and he attended Willamette University and then "college in Philadelphia." As early as mid-1906, the partners established an office in Portland, which Legg appears to have manned while his family remained in Salem (and he maintained it post-partnership until 1915 or 1916).[175] Through this office, presumably, the firm took on a number of projects in Portland and nearby, including two public schools in 1907, one in St. Johns (now a Portland district) and the other in Carlton, west of Portland; two hotels and inns; a Masonic temple (East Portland); several commercial buildings; and two upscale private homes.[176] Most of these design projects were at least engaged before the end of 1907.[177] The building contractors for these projects were varied; however, both school projects were built by the firm of Welch & Mourer, Pugh's collaborators in the construction of both the Eugene and Salem high schools. The Salem school, though built after the debut of the partnership, was designed and approved prior, and Pugh, as noted, superintended its construction. The first Pugh & Legg–designed school building was a one-story frame building in School District 61, Polk County. The call for bids went out on August 27, 1905.[178]

This considerable run of high school building projects, all in the first decade of the twentieth century, was testimony to the fact that high school had become a generalized component of public education in Oregon for the first time in legislation passed in 1901. There were three times as many high schools in Oregon in 1908 as there were in 1900, and they had a 131 percent increase in enrollment from 1901 to 1908.[179] Here, once again, the firm of Pugh, and then Pugh & Legg, was in the right place at the right time.

The division of labor in their partnership on many of the design projects is not discernible—with certain documented exceptions. It does seem likely that Legg was chiefly responsible for procuring projects in Portland and its orbit, and therefore, he probably drew the plans for those projects as well. By the same token, it seems likely that Pugh continued to retain and draw plans for most of the jobs in Salem and the Central Valley area. "Architects: Pugh & Legg" was a standard designation for those years, beginning in July 1905. Until May, at any rate, Pugh was still running his habitual advertisement in local papers: "W.D. Pugh—architect and superintendent, plans furnished for all classes of building and structural work. Office 116 State Street, Tioga Block, Salem, Oregon."[180]

Apparently the first "Plan drawn by Architects Pugh & Legg" was for the medical college building on the campus of Willamette University. On July 19, the *Capital Journal* reported:

> *The final plans and specifications have been adopted for the new medical building for Willamette University....The plans, as drawn by Architects Pugh & Legg, were adopted* [last night at a meeting of the finance committee], *and bids will be advertised for at once. The building will be constructed of brick and will cost, complete, outside of equipment, etc., about $15,000.*[181]

The report continued with a description of the building, according to the adopted plans. The basement was to be used as a chemical laboratory, the first floor proper was for classrooms, the second floor was for lecture rooms and the spacious attic was for a "dissecting and clinic room." In all, it would comprise fourteen thousand square feet. The Beaux-Arts-style brick building was to be located in the northwest corner of the campus, about a hundred feet from State and Winter Streets, respectively.[182] The building was ready for occupancy in February 1906.

College of Medicine, Willamette University (1905). *Image courtesy of Willamette University Archives and Special Collections.*

The medical college building and the medical school for which it was built have an interesting and rather complicated history. At present, the building houses the art and art history departments, and it has been much expanded on the east side. It is the second-oldest building on campus, just after Waller Hall.[183] The College of Medicine at Willamette was created as early as 1867 on the Salem campus. In 1880, it was moved to Portland. Then, in 1895, it moved back to the Salem campus, apparently due to a dispute over clinical privileges at the Portland hospital. It was lodged, as before, in Waller Hall, but it used other buildings in the area as well. From there, in 1906, it moved into the new Pugh & Legg–designed building. Finally, in 1913, the College of Medicine merged with the Medical School of the University of Oregon in Portland. The medical school was then located in northwest Portland on the campus of Good Samaritan Hospital. In 1919, the medical school relocated to its present site in southwest Portland and is now known as Oregon Health & Science University (OHSU).

Following the merger of the medical college with the University of Oregon's College of Medicine, the campus building was then occupied by the law school, its first regular home on campus, where it remained until Gatke Hall was moved to campus in 1938. The building, in this period, was also home to the science department, appropriately enough, but it was also home to the academic department, or Willamette Academy. The academy was closed in 1916, as it had been rendered superfluous by the generalized development of public high school education in the region.[184] The science department moved to a new building in 1941, and the music department moved in, where it remained until 1976, when, following extensive remodeling, the art department moved in, and the building was renamed the art building. In 2002, a large wing was attached on the east side, with walkways connecting it to the original building on all three floors.[185]

Another significant early project of the Pugh & Legg era was the Benton County State Bank Building, or Johnson Bank, after its founder Archie J. Johnson, as it was generally known; it was later known as the Madison Building (National Register of Historic Places no. 79002035.) The plans for the building were accepted in late August 1906, and its doors were opened on July 25, 1907. Its appearance and proportions are close to those of the Roseburg bank job of 1902: two-story buff-brick corner building with a main

Benton County National Bank, Corvallis, Oregon (1906). *Photograph by Angelus Studios, courtesy of University of Oregon Libraries, Special Collections and University Archives.*

A man with a wagon full of corn in front of Benton County National Bank. *Sydney Trask Photograph Collection, courtesy of Oregon State University, Special Collections and Archives Research Center, Corvallis Historical Images.*

entrance on the corner and a brick decorative cornice under the eaves. The nomination form describes it as a building "in the Richardsonian tradition," perhaps because of the large arched window openings on the ground story. (In subsequent remodeling, as in Roseburg, the corner bay entrance was removed, although the large granite columns, which were much admired by the press when installed, remain.) Archie Johnson, the president and builder of the bank, was from a Marion County pioneer family and had a profile rather similar to that of Booth of the Roseburg bank—only, his valley background, of course, was less in timber and more in agriculture. He was involved in everything from farming and stock-raising to real estate, general merchandising, wool, mohair brokering and milling and lumber. He was a national bank examiner for five Pacific Northwest states, a councilman and mayor of Corvallis at the time of the bank's construction and a state senator for thirty years, ending in 1924.[186]

Between 1906 and 1907, Pugh & Legg were credited with designing the plans for the following Portland buildings, in addition to the school buildings (dates of registry in *Portland Daily Abstract*):

- Store building at Southeast Sixth Avenue, at or near Southeast Hawthorne Boulevard (November 23, 1906).
- Hotel for James Olson on Grand Avenue, at or near Southeast Hawthorne Boulevard (Sargents Hotel) (January 4, 1907).
- Mixed multi-residence and store on East Thirty-Fourth Street, at or near Hawthorne Boulevard (January 8, 1907).
- W.H. Lang Hotel on Southwest Front Avenue, at or near Southwest Harrison Street (possibly Hotel Harrison) (January 29, 1907).
- Goldstein building at 405 Southwest First Avenue. (May 25, 1907).
- Apartments for Mrs. T. Halverson, Southeast Main Street, between Southeast Thirteenth and Southeast Fourteenth Avenues (June 26, 1907).
- East Portland Masonic Temple, Southeast Eighth Avenue at the southwest corner of East Burnside Street (December 23, 1907).

Left: Sargent Hotel, Hawthorne and Grand Streets, Portland, Oregon (1907). *Photograph by Angelus Studio, courtesy of the University of Oregon Libraries, Special Collections and University Archives.*

Right: Hotel Harrison, at the corner of Southwest Front Avenue and Southwest Harrison Street, Portland, Oregon (1906). *Photograph by Angelus Studio, Courtesy of the University of Oregon Libraries, Special Collections and University Archives.*

They were also credited with designing two residences:

- Louise Fritz, two-story frame in Sunnyside, Portland (November 3, 1906).
- F.P. Waring, single-family residence, two-story frame, Northeast Weidler Street, between Northeast Seventeenth and Northeast Eighteenth Avenues (June 12, 1907).[187]

The two private residences built in Portland from plans provided by the firm of Pugh & Legg in the period between 1906 and 1909 stand in contrast to the number of buildings the firm designed in Salem and the surrounding area in the same period—or, more precisely, in 1907–8. In this period, they built no less than eight residences, six in 1908 alone. The Portland-area market was already occupied by a number of well-established architectural firms, of course.[188] The significant increase in the number of contracts for the design of private residences in the Salem area at that time—there had been only one or two per year in the 1890s and none since 1900—may have been due, in part, to the increased capacity of the new partnership. It may also be due, in part, to the fact that the "Index, Summaries of Buildings by Names of Architect/Designers" of the *Portland Daily Abstract* covers only the years between 1906 and 1909 (that is, roughly coterminous with the Pugh & Legg partnership). In other words, there may have been more residential design projects before and after those recorded here.

In 1907, two private residences in Salem were listed as "designs in progress" by Pugh & Legg:

- Zadoc Riggs's house (April 24, 1907).
- Mayor Rodgers's house on the northwest corner of Cottage and Court Streets (April 24, 1907).

And 1908 "designs in progress":

- John Bayne house (April 8, 1908).
- William Brown house (April 8, 1908).
- Willis S. Duniway house (April 11, 1908).
- Mrs. S.C. Dyer house (April 8, 1908).
- Ray L. Farmer house on the corner of Thirteenth and Center Streets, on the south side of Center Street (April 8, 1908).
- C.H. Hinges house (April 8, 1908).

The cost estimates for these houses were in the $2,500 to $4,000 range.

The years 1907 and 1908 brought several significant state projects and one county project to the firm. In March 1907, the *Capital Journal* reported, "Walter Pugh, of Salem, was chosen as architect to the [insane] asylum. He is the only resident architect of Salem and put up the other wings."[189] Bids were solicited, and plans, specifications and instructions were sent to bidders to be examined in the governor's office or the office of W.D. Pugh. The contract for the construction of the new wing, an eastern extension of the north wing specially designed for housing the criminally insane (bars instead of grating on the windows, et cetera), was awarded to Salem contractors Welch & Mourer at a cost of $83,885. All work was to be terminated by December 1, 1907, but additional time was allowed for unavoidable delays.[190] The *Daily Abstract* listed this job as a Pugh & Legg project, although Legg's name is mentioned nowhere in connection with it. In terms of building costs, this was probably the largest architectural project of Pugh's career, second only to the firm's design of the U.S. National Bank building in 1909, which, in its turn, it seems, was primarily a Legg project.

The J building corpus of the Oregon State Hospital, showing the north extension. *Courtesy of the Oregon Historical Society Research Library.*

The west façade of the J building, Oregon State Hospital. *Photograph by Josh Partee, Creative Commons Attribution, Share Alike 2.5, generic license.*

By the same token, the principal projects of 1908, apart from the private residences listed above—the buildings of the State Institution for the Feeble-Minded and Epileptic (Fairview Training Center and Fairview Home) and the Crook County Courthouse in Prineville—seem to have been entirely Pugh projects.

Pugh's name first appears in connection with the state's condemnation of the Thiel Farm, southeast of Salem, for the construction of the Fairview Center. As a state's witness, before the jury that was impaneled to consider the case, Pugh was introduced as the "state architect for the new institution."[191] The purpose of the new Oregon State Institution for the Feeble-Minded, created by legislation in 1907, was to "educate the feeble-minded" and care for "the idiotic and epileptic." Its 670 acres, once cleared, were mainly devoted to a working farm "that provided both food and training for its residents."[192] The call for bids for the various construction jobs at Fairview listed Pugh's Salem office, along with the secretary of state's office in the capitol building, as places where the plans, specifications and instructions could be consulted. It sometimes added, for that purpose, Fred A. Legg's office at Third and Oak Streets in Portland.

The building contract for the five buildings—administration building, dormitory, laundry, boiler house and barn—went to the low bid of $47,405 from H.N. Eley. Fairview decided to use the existing barn for the time being, so the total came down to $41,285. The steam heating and plumbing contracts went to Theo. M. Barr (heating, $10,245) and Bernardi & Dunsford (plumbing, $1,895). Pugh was instructed to draw up the required contract for the completion of the buildings no later than December 1.

The most attractive and noticeable among these buildings was LeBreton Cottage, a Colonial Revival frame building comprising 23,184 square feet; it served as the administration building and also, for several years, as the girls' dormitory. Pugh designed the buildings and the layout for the entire facility, but he did not superintend the construction of the four buildings, no doubt due to the number of buildings being put up at once, with separate contractors for heating and plumbing and so on.[193] So, H.E. Bickers was hired as the superintendent of construction for a salary of $1,500 per year. Once construction was far enough along, in 1908, the first patients were transferred from the state insane asylum. Buildings were added, and the population of "inmates," as they were called for decades, grew. "In 1981, there were more than 1,300 Oregonians with developmental disabilities liv[ing] at the Fairview Training Center."[194] In the early 1920s, eugenics legislation provided for the "sterilization of all feeble-minded, insane, epileptics, habitual criminals, moral degenerates and sexual perverts who

Le Breton Hall (administration building and dormitory), Fairview Center, Oregon Institution for the Feeble Minded, Salem, Oregon (1908). *Image courtesy of Willamette University, Archives and Special Collections.*

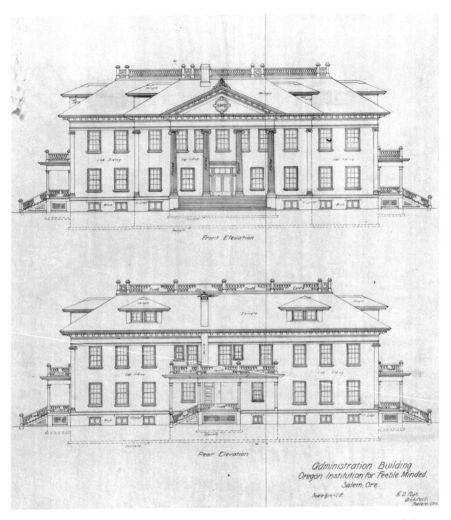

Le Breton Hall, architect's elevations (front and rear) by W.D. Pugh (1908). *Courtesy of the Oregon State Archives.*

are a menace to society." Sterilizations required either the person's consent or a court order. A system of "parole" was established in 1931 to homes or elsewhere for work. All "parolees" had to be sterilized. The facility was finally closed in 2000. "Sustainable community" developments bought some of the property and used some of the historic buildings for a time. The last of the original buildings were demolished in 2016.

Shortly after the contracts for the Fairview facilities were distributed, Pugh was reportedly on a visit to Eugene in the company of his recent collaborator,

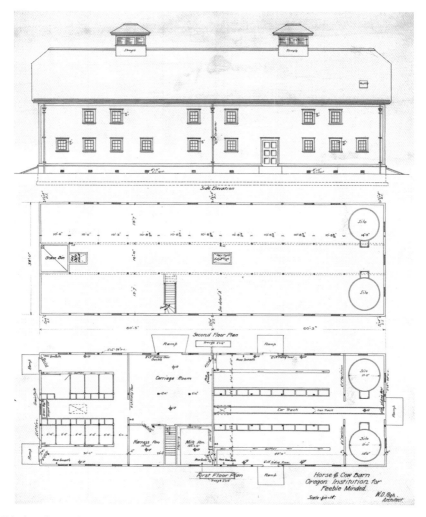

Fairview Center horse and cow barn, architect's side elevation and two floorplans by W.D. Pugh (1908). *Courtesy of the Oregon State Archives.*

contractor G.C. Mourer, "looking after some big buildings, which are to be erected in Eugene this summer."[195] And earlier that year, in February, the *Statesman Journal* reported, "Fred A. Legg, of Portland, and contractor W.M. Welch of this city," Mourer's recent partner on the school projects, were ready to proceed with the construction of "the new Breyman building, which is to be erected on Court Street in the near future [and] is to be one of Salem's handsomest business blocks."[196] There is no mention of Pugh, who was something of a specialist on building blocks in downtown Salem.

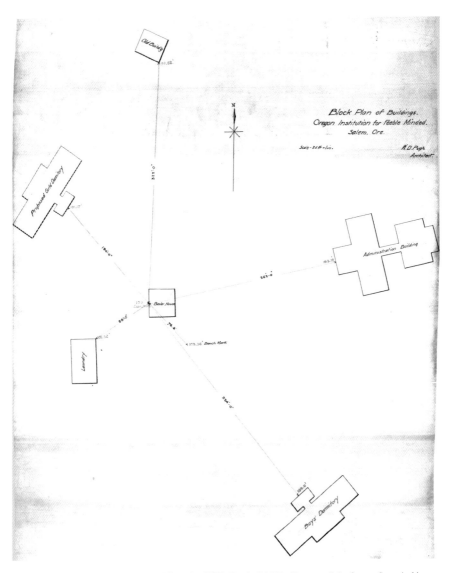

Fairview Center, block plan of buildings by W.D. Pugh (1908). *Courtesy of the Oregon State Archives.*

Indeed, it appears that Pugh and Legg were maintaining separate shops alongside their mutual venture all along. As early as mid-1906, Pugh alone had drawn up and accepted plans for an imposing courthouse for Crook County in Prineville. The elevations and floor plans are preserved in the Crook County clerk's office. They are signed by Pugh alone.[197]

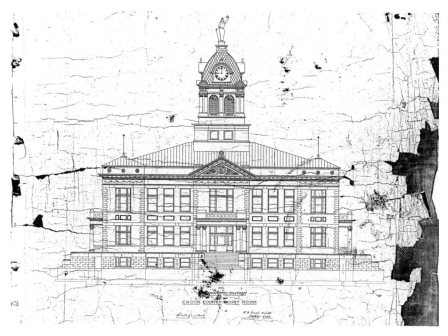

Crook County Courthouse, Prineville, Oregon. Architect's front elevation by W.D. Pugh (1908; first plans submitted in 1906). *Courtesy of the Crook County clerk's office.*

Crook County Courthouse, Prineville, Oregon. Architect's side elevation by W. D. Pugh (1906 and 1908). *Courtesy of the Crook County clerk's office.*

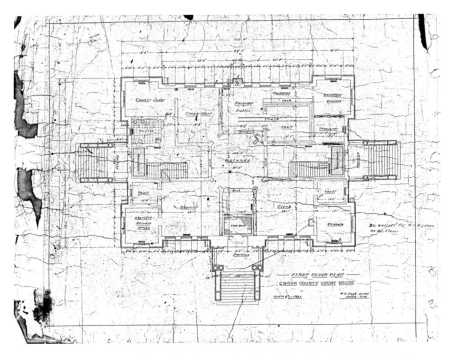

Crook County Courthouse, Prineville, Oregon. Architect's first floorplan by W.D. Pugh (1906 and 1908). *Courtesy of the Crook County clerk's office.*

The Pugh-designed Crook County Courthouse was completed in May 1909. The county had already accepted a bid for a total of $75,000 in 1906, but residents protested and obtained an injunction "on the grounds that the building would incur unwanted indebtedness. This against a background of complaints about high taxes and bad roads."[198] In 1907, a lower bid from Wright and McNeely, a Portland firm, was accepted. They defaulted after building the above-ground basement and some staircases. It seems reasonable to assume that this had something to do with their defaulting, especially in light of the fact that, in the end, the total cost of the building came to just a few dollars under $75,000, not counting the almost $1,000 of labor and material donated by the contractors.[199] A new main building contract was awarded to J.B. Shipp, a local lumber executive, builder and civic leader, who completed the job.

What had been undertaken to confirm Prineville's position as the most important city in north-central Oregon in anticipation of the railroad's arrival to connect the region's resources—especially timber—with the wider world, backfired. "Disgruntled residents of northern and western

Crook County began to grumble about having to support a 'Taj Mahal' in Prineville. The grumblings eventually led to the residents of northern Crook County petitioning to have a new county created from the northern part of Crook. In 1914, a vote led to the creation of Jefferson County from Crook. Residents of Bend, Redmond and Sisters also attempted to create a new county from western and southern Crook County, but the votes failed the first time around. The residents of Bend tried to have the county seat moved from Prineville to Bend, since they could not have their own county. Apparently, this threat allowed enough votes to be garnered for the creation of Deschutes County from Crook County in 1916. Deschutes was the last county created in Oregon.[200] In that same year, the fate of Prineville's aspirations to be a major rail hub were sealed when the Oregon Trunk Line, operated by Harriman and Hill interests, bypassed Prineville on its way from the Columbia to Redmond and Bend and eventually to a rail connection with California through Klamath Falls. The citizens of Prineville had to vote on a bond issue to build a feeder line to the trunk.[201]

At the time of its construction, the courthouse was one of the tallest buildings in Oregon. It has been called central Oregon's best-known building. Its clock tower commands a panoramic view of the Ochoco Valley and can be seen for miles around. Its original interior arrangements, in their rational displacement of offices and departments, are reminiscent of Salem City Hall. The exterior remains mostly unchanged, although two broad flights of steps on the east and west sides have been removed. Pugh received a fee of $1,700 for his services.[202] By some minor irony of fate, Pugh was living in Deschutes County when it broke off from gigantic Crook County, in some measure because of the construction of the imposing courthouse that he had designed ten years earlier.

In May 1908, the *Statesman Journal* announced that plans and specifications for the Liberty (south Salem) school building were ready for examination in the office of Pugh & Legg, Architects, Salem.[203] And on June 12, 1908, the paper carried a headline in huge block letters on the center of page 1: "NEW FIVE-STORY STEEL BUILDING WILL BE ERECTED ON COMMERCIAL STREET AT ONCE. United States National Bank will Proceed to the Erection of a Modern Steel Fire-Proof Structure Without Delay—75 Office Rooms in Upper Stories Have Already Been Rented—Architects Are Now Drawing Plans—Other Skyscrapers Expected to Follow." The architects were listed as Pugh & Legg, "who are busily engaged now on the plans for the mammoth structure. They will complete their work in about ten days." This five-story modern steel construction marked "a new

Crook County Courthouse, Prineville, Oregon (1908). *Courtesy of www.Keith@courthousehistory.com.*

era in the development of Salem."[204] Many details, then already available, followed: fireproofing, elevators, et cetera. The oversubscription of tenants for the seventy-five offices showed that "the city's business and professional men have metropolitan tastes."[205]

The "skyscraper" was reportedly under construction on the corner of Commercial and State Streets by the end of May 1909, and it was due for completion on December 12. By the time of its completion, if not before, the design of the U.S. Bank Building in Salem was regularly attributed to Legg alone. A photograph of the just-completed building, showing construction debris still scattered around it, is labeled: "F.A. Legg, Architect." But in June 1908, when its construction was first reported, it had been labeled a Pugh & Legg enterprise. And a substantial article in the *Statesman Journal* on January 1, 1909, "PUGH & LEGG ARE LEADING ARCHITECTS," begins:

Among the leading architects of the state is the firm of Pugh & Legg, who have offices in the Murphy building, Salem, Oregon, and also in the Ainsworth building, Portland, Oregon. The high class of work of this firm will be seen in various parts of the state.... They are now doing practically [all] of the architectural work in this locality. Their work for the coming year promises to be very good, as they are working on plans for some very

Above: *Oregon Main Street: A Rephotographic Study*, by James Norman. *Center left*: U.S. National Bank Building (1909). *Courtesy of the Oregon Historical Society Research Library, OHS I.D. NOM57.*

Left: U.S. National Bank/ Pioneer Trust, 109–117 Northeast Commercial Street (1908–1909). *Photograph by Thomas N. Green Jr., courtesy of SHINE on Salem, Salem Heritage Network.*

substantial buildings to be erected in the spring. There are already many monuments to this firm in Salem, most of the pretentious buildings of the city having been designed by them.[206]

On May 19, the newspapers carried the announcement that Pugh & Legg were accepting bids for the Liberty School building.[207] And then, on May 30, the *Statesman Journal* carried a large article: "BUILDING TO BE OF THE BEST, Describing in Detail Just How the New National Bank Building Will Be Constructed." The details of both the interior arrangements, materials and structure followed: "The general construction of the building is to be of concrete, steel, stone and brick and will represent an expenditure of $100,000. Pugh & Legg of Salem are the architects, and the Northwestern Bridge Company of Portland have the contract for construction." Details of the ground-floor corner location of the bank proper, "26 feet on Commercial, 100 feet on State," its vault, et cetera, were all given, again, with details that indicate familiarity with the plans and specifications, which, of course, had to have been provided for the bidding that had already been won by Northwestern Bridge.[208]

Ten days later, on June 11, the same paper carried an announcement that plans and specifications for the construction of the administration building, boiler house and dormitory for the school for the deaf were "ready for builders at the office of F.A. Legg, Architect."[209] And the day after that, the *Capital Journal* printed this news under the title "Two Fine Buildings:

> *Walter D. Pugh, the well-known Salem architect, who, on account of his poor health, has taken up contracting, was the successful bidder on two fine buildings to be erected at the Institution for Feeble Minded and Epileptics.... The two identical frame* [dormitory] *buildings, with brick basement, 43 x 124 feet, will cost $29,442....The state will do the excavating and grading and furnish the brick with convict labor* [standard procedure for state building projects at the time]. *As an architect, Mr. Pugh enjoys a splendid reputation, having planned some of the most important public buildings in this city and state. His work stands the test from a structural standpoint. With such an equipment, Mr. Pugh is splendidly qualified to undertake contracting. His health is improving with outdoor life. The plans for these buildings were made by Charles Burggraf, the well-known Albany architect.*[210]

Burggraf had been Pugh's competitor for a number of design projects for public buildings. Thus, Pugh was both the "architect of the institution" at is establishment and, later, contractor for two of its buildings.

Two dormitories were built several years later, based on plans provided by Legg: Kozer Cottage, a 15,312-square-foot building constructed in 1920 as a residence for infants, and Smith cottage, a 19,074-square-foot building constructed as a girls' dormitory in 1921.

In fact, Pugh had gotten back into the contracting business as early as May 1908. "W.D. Pugh is building two [new dwellings] fronting on Waller Street, between Twelfth and Thirteenth Streets, at a cost of about $1,500 each, both of which are already rented." These houses, finished by June 20, appear to have been built as Pugh's personal investments. Then came an announcement in November 1908, revealing that Pugh has gotten back into the contracting business—at that time, for the construction of roads, streets and bridges—with a Mr. Herren as partner.[211]

Then, punctuated by at least one "Pugh & Legg" project—a garage and stable for "Messrs. Brownstein & Son" at the very end of the year—and the January 1, 1909 encomium "Pugh & Legg Are Leading Architects," the papers reported on the contract for a new South Commercial Street Bridge over Mill Creek; with a bid of $4,649, it was awarded to Pugh and Herren.[212] After the announcement of Pugh's contract for the two Fairview buildings at mid-year, a number of road and street paving jobs followed: improvements to Winter Street, from State Street all the way to the fairgrounds; Kearny Street; South Water Street Bridge; and so on, into 1910.

This shift from architecture to contracting, especially road and street contracting, will be addressed in the following chapter. It seems reasonably clear that a lack of architectural work was not an issue here—at least if the local press is to be believed. The *Statesman Journal* ran a large piece titled "Big Growth of the City" at the end of September 1909. After recounting the "enormous expenditures" of that year so far, which amounted to "something over $1,872,448.20 [*sic*]," it was predicted that the year's total would be $2.5 million (including the bank building, asylum and Fairview Center, state library, schools, etc.).

> *Any doubt as to the correctness of the figures given will be dispelled by reference to the architects and contractors of this city. The architects are working night and day and have been all summer trying to turn out orders they have for plans and specifications. All of the contractors here and others from other cities who are doing work in Salem are completely snowed under with the immense volume of building.*

The article went on to quote F.A. Legg, one of the prominent architects of the city, who, when asked about the large increase in building, stated that "this was only the beginning.…Mr. Legg expects that the coming year will see double the amount of building done than what will be completed by the end of 1909."[213]

By the end of 1909, according to both Salem papers, Legg had already taken Pugh's place as Salem's number-one architect. The *Statesman Journal* ran the headline: "Salem Architect Wins Reputation." The article stated,

"Mr. Fred A. Legg, known as 'Salem's architect,' is known throughout the Northwest as the most proficient workman of his trade. He has been a resident of Salem, Oregon, from time to time, for twenty-five years, several years of which he and Mr. Pugh of this city were partners in business." The article goes on to list his accomplishments:

- *The plans and designs for the U.S. National Bank.*
- *The buildings of the mute school.*
- *The new Garfield School ("the most artistic public school in Marion County").*
- *The new arcade at the Oregon State Fair.*
- *The big barn at the insane asylum ("the best barn in the West").*

It concluded, "At present, he is working on the plans and designs of the Union Bank & Trust in Portland, twelve-stories high."[214] The new Breyman Block might have been added.

Much the same litany was repeated in the January 1, 1910 issue of the *Capital Journal*, which added the H.S. Gill & Co. warehouse and offices, the Eppley and Fullerton residences in Salem and the Portland-Burlington warehouse and dock and three grain elevators in Portland.[215]

A postcard of the Oregon School for the Deaf on Locust Street, Salem, Oregon, 1912. *PH Collection 801, courtesy of the University of Washington Libraries, Special Collections Division.*

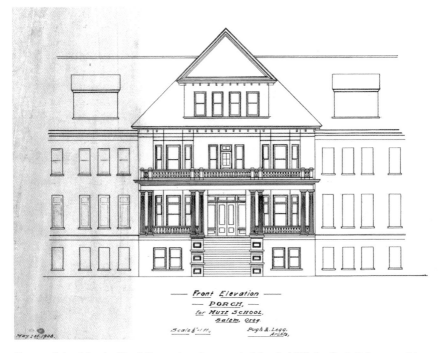

Oregon School for the Deaf. Front elevation, porch, May 1, 1908, by Pugh & Legg, architects. *Courtesy of the Oregon State Archives.*

Already, in April 1909, an article on the state's purchase of fifty-four acres north of town for the site of the new deaf school declared, "Fred Legg, the state architect, has all his plans in readiness and building operations will begin at an early day."[216] The elevations and plans preserved in the Oregon State Archives, however, are all signed "Pugh & Legg, Archts."

Walter Pugh's long run as Salem's premier architect was, nevertheless, over.

HITTING THE ROAD

When W.D. Pugh turned from architecture to contracting for the second time, he did so more exclusively, and he primarily went in the direction of road and street work—especially paving. In fact, after completing the contract for the construction of the two big frame dormitories at the Fairview Home in mid-1909, he did not appear to undertake any significant building contracts for some time, although he bid on the construction of a school house in the Englewood District in March 1910 (his bid of $24,887 lost out to a bid of $23,800 by his sometime collaborator G.C. Mourer).[217] In March 1911, he bid on the construction of an addition to the high school.[218] In February 1912, he submitted a bid for the construction of two schoolhouses in the Richmond and Highland additions, respectively, but he subsequently withdrew it.[219] It was not until 1922 that he took on, with a partner, the construction of a new Methodist old person's home.[220] He ran a classified advertisement for a time in the mid-1920s in the "Contractor-Building" category. And a few design jobs were taken on by architect W.D. Pugh in the late 1910s and 1920s, including another bank job and a building for the Salem branch of a large fruit company's operations.

But for a good five years, between 1909 and 1914, Pugh was one of the several Salem competitors vying for the suddenly numerous road building and, especially, paving contracts in a surge of activity that was provoked by the arrival of automobiles and motorcycles, kicking up dust as they came. This surge was comparable, in some measure, to the railroad rush of the 1870s–90s.[221] For several years, the Salem newspapers were peppered with stories about bids for street and bridge jobs, discussions of the relative merits of asphalt (macadamized) and concrete, of crushed rock versus gravel concrete and so on. The city, exercising assessments to home and other urban property owners based on length of street frontage, was putting out contracts for road and street paving with great speed.

One of the vehicles that was kicking up dust belonged to W.D. Pugh, whose name appears as the owner of a Hendee Mfg. motorcycle (later known as the Indian motorcycle) on a 1909 list of Salem people with "auto and motorcycle licenses issued by the secretary of state." The following year, W.D. Pugh had graduated to an Oldsmobile.[222] A brief examination of Pugh's involvement in Salem's paving boom is needed before confronting the question of why he so abruptly shifted his gears to the road and street contracting business.

Between March 1909 and the end of 1913, W.D. Pugh put in no fewer than forty bids for street improvements, mainly concrete paving; they were mostly in Salem, but there were also a few in Albany, Corvallis and Stayton. These bids—with estimates generally based on the square yards of concrete, crushed rock or gravel required—ranged from $1,000 or so to more than $20,000. For example, his bid for the paving of Market Street included several estimates based on different materials: $20,285.05 (crushed rock or concrete), $19,495.45 (six-inch-grade concrete), $14,685.56 (six-inch crushed rock) and $13,896.96 (six-inch gravel).[223] Of these, Pugh came in with low bids and got the jobs for at least fourteen projects, possibly more, since the local press did not always follow up on the awarding of contracts. According to an article in the Albany paper reporting on a spring 1911 visit by Pugh, who was in town to drum up interest in his product ("cement concrete hard surface pavement"), "Mr. Pugh…laid 20,000 square yards last year."[224] Perhaps the largest concrete paving job of this period was Marion Street: "Property owners of Marion street, last evening [April 10, 1913] at a city hall mass meeting, decided to pave with concrete and indorsed the tender of W.D. Pugh, his bid, $21,996.64 being the lowest."[225] The largest job in the general category of infrastructure that Pugh bid on in this period was for the construction of the North Salem Sewer System; he bid $93,000, which lost out to that of A. Burns, a contractor from Spokane, Washington.[226]

Most of the street, road and infrastructure building competition was local, involving three or four firms, including Pugh's, and it was intense. In the sewer contract bid that was just mentioned, for example, after losing out to Burns for the lowest bid, Pugh offered, after the bids were made public, to revise his bid down by 7 percent, but this offer "was turned down flatly by the unanimous vote of the [city] council."[227] In May 1913, the *Capital Journal* ran a piece titled "Is There a Paving Combine?" The article reported on a "pretty noisy rumor in general circulation" that there had been a paving combine in operation for some time:

> *It is claimed that, instead of bidding against each other, that every contract is apportioned out in advance. Every company or bidder, says the rumor… is told what the successful bid is to be and that his bid must be enough higher to be certain of being shut out. By this simple arrangement, each company would, of course, get its contract in turn, and the business be divided between them amicably and at their own prices.*

The newspaper, it was claimed, knew nothing of such a combine, only of the rumor. But "certain persons" were said to be keeping tabs on the contracts, and they held that a regular rotation of contracts would indicate that such a combine really exists. The article continued:

> [In the meantime], *paving goes merrily on, and it is probable by the time all the streets are paved, which will not be long, the first ones paved will be ready for a new paving…and we will have it all to do over again. Thus, will our lives be made one joyous round of gladsome paving contracts, interspersed occasionally with a sewer or two as a sort of side dish at the paving feast. However, if there is any truth in this rumor…it will crop out sooner or later, because if companies or men will combine to cinch the public, a smaller portion will combine to cinch the balance of the combine, and then there will be trouble.*[228]

The author of the article was on the right track, of course; it did "crop out" but not quite in the way they had imagined. Ten days later, on May 27, the same paper ran a big story, "A Paving Story That Lasted Quick." A paving combine had recently been put into execution by three leading Salem paving contractors—namely, W.D. Pugh, Arenz & Co. and August Kehrberger. The three had agreed that one of the largest paving contracts ever let in the city were to go to Kehrberger, who drew the North Commercial Street job. Pugh drew Chemeketa Street, while Arenz & Co. drew Twenty-First Street. Sure enough, as predicted, one of the trio, Arenz, broke the pact and underbid Kehrberger for the North Commercial Street job. But Arenz did not get the job either, as they were underbid by the Geiger Construction Company, which had not participated in the lottery because Geiger, who was back east when the call for bids went out, heard about it, rushed back to Salem and produced a winning bid. He was, if not unaware of, at least outside the "combine" and free to bid as he chose. (The article rather implies that Geiger was no stranger to "combinations.")[229]

There was no more combining; the practice had apparently been in place for only a short while, and the citizenry was probably not taken to the cleaners by this "cinch." All bids had to be pretty close to job estimates made by the city engineer, which, by their nature, tended to the parsimonious. It may be that the "combines" were essentially a means of avoiding underbidding to the point of nonprofitability for the contractors involved. Perhaps it was understood by the city administration and other interested parties, which may explain why there were no legal or, apparently, practical consequences suffered by the combiners; they all went on bidding and getting paving jobs for some time.

No serious issues regarding fulfillment of contracts by W.D. Pugh were reported by the newspapers in this period of considerable activity. On July 22, 1910, the *Oregonian* reported, "A clash between the Marion County Court and Walter Pugh, a leading contractor and prominent citizen, caused a special session of the court here [Salem] today and may result in the arrest of Pugh tomorrow." (The district attorney was unable to secure a warrant that day because the judge was absent). It was alleged that Pugh had been taking hundreds of dollars' worth of crushed rock from the county rock quarry "without warrant of authority" for paving Winter Street, one of the main residential thoroughfares. County judge William Busher claimed that Pugh had asked permission from the court to take the rock, but that permission had been refused. It was further claimed that Pugh had operated the rock crusher without county authority.[230] The *Statesman Journal* reported the same story, adding that "the county court has become incensed over the attitude shown and intend to take some action leading to a settlement."[231] Some kind of reasonably amicable settlement must have been reached in this affair, as the press (searchable and digitized) made no further mention of it, and Pugh went right on getting paving contracts from the city. Aside from several rather routine suits in both directions for unpaid building materials balances, unpaid extra paving work and the like, the paving of Salem's streets proceeded smoothly—except for one incident on a Pugh job, as it turns out.

In May 1912, according to a story in the *Capital Journal*, some fifty workers at an excavation job for the Hubbard building at the corner of High and State Streets went on strike for higher wages (the men were getting $0.20 an hour, or $2.00 for a ten-hour day, and men with teams were paid $4.50 per day). The workmen were demanding $2.50 for an eight-hour day, and the team drivers were demanding $5.00 per day. The contractor, W.D. Pugh, refused these demands, so the teams dumped the dirt that had already been loaded. Work was resumed the following day with a small crew of men at the old wage; this was done amid accusations, which were accepted by the newspaper reporter and denied by the strikers, of Industrial Workers of the World (IWW) agitation. On the second day of the strike, according to the newspaper account, twenty more men either quit or were dismissed by the contractor for being "Wobblies." According to the *Capital Journal* report, "The contractor is endeavoring to secure other men to take the place of the strikers."[232]

According to a *Statesman Journal* account of the next day, Pugh declared there had been no strike, only trouble arising from the demand of three teamsters that all teams get a raise to five dollars per day. Their refusal to work left the excavating crew with nothing to do. They were approached by members of the IWW who urged them to join the teamsters on strike, but none of them went on strike, according to one interviewed worker. They waited until 2:00 p.m. and then left when it began to rain.[233] The readiness of the local newspapers to see IWW agitation in these trades is not far from normal. The year 1912 saw a great deal of IWW activity, strikes and demonstrations up and down the West Coast. On the same day that the teamsters struck at the Pugh operation, Oregon Electric workers who were laying tracks between Salem and Eugene went on an IWW-led strike for better wages, hours and food amid rumors that the IWW intended to dynamite one of the Southern Pacific's bridges.[234] It is not clear how the matter at the Hubbard site was resolved—with wage increase for the teamsters or with their replacement—for it was not reported in the papers. Nor were there other reports at the time of IWW agitation or recruiting in the ongoing Salem paving/infrastructure activity.

By the fall of 1913, indeed as early as August, Pugh was winding down his Salem paving jobs and turning to road building opportunities in the state of Washington, in partnership with G.C. Arenz, one of his competitors throughout the Salem street paving race. Before we proceed to that period in W.D. Pugh's enterprises, the question of his rather sharp turn from architecture to paving and road building in 1909 begs to be addressed. In doing so, we are obliged to rely almost entirely on the evidence of his actions, in view of the almost total lack of written narrative sources about motives, such as memoirs and correspondence—both genres in which neither the Pughs nor the Hobsons appear to have been much inclined to indulge. Those who, no doubt, could have provided enlightenment on this question, alas, are gone, as, indeed, are many others who may have had conversations with them on this subject.

One exception to this rule is a letter, dated September 30, 1995, that was written to the author from Walter and Jessie's oldest daughter, Katherine (1903–2010). The letter is printed as appendix B. In this letter, Katherine muses about her father's architectural career, why he gave it up and why family members, including herself, knew so little about it:

> *Maybe memories were painful to Dad. He had enjoyed prestige, was a state architect during Gov. Penoyer's* [sic] *term and had made lots of money, then decided that his eyes were not as good and decided to work out of* [i.e., outside of] *his office and be a contractor.*

Katherine's observation echoes, to a point, the June 1909 editorial quoted in chapter 4, that announced Pugh was taking up contracting "on account of his poor health." But its concluding remark, that "his health is improving with outdoor life," does not confirm, at least, that his health issue was failing eyesight. There is some evidence that much earlier in his career, in the early 1890s, he may have had a problem with alcohol or some other form of substance abuse; however, the most productive period of his architectural career was still ahead of him at that point, and there is no further evidence of that kind.[235] Of course, there may have been other health issues at play.

Changing fashion and technology in architecture is another matter worth attention regarding Walter Pugh's turn in 1909 to road and paving contracting. The structural materials with which he had dealt as an architect were frame and, especially for larger public and commercial buildings, brick. One might say that brick was his signature medium, as it was—or had been—for countless other architects and builders. Architects of this period could rely on detailed construction guides, such as Samuel Sloan's *City and Suburban Architecture*, which was first published in Philadelphia in 1859 and reissued in 1867.[236] In matters of style, Pugh hewed to established classical models. Perhaps the new skyscraper technology of steel and concrete was unappealing to his artistic tastes, as exemplified by the last big project with which he was at least formally involved, the U.S. Bank Building. Perhaps, as an architect friend of the author noted on examining a list and a few plans and elevations of buildings designed by Pugh, there was an element of "burnout" in his decision to turn away from architecture after so many years of intensive work of that kind.[237]

In 1905, the National Board of Fire Underwriters had created the national building code to minimize risk to property and building occupants. In 1907, the first state bill requiring the registration of engineers was passed in Wyoming. These innovations led, in due course, to the establishment of boards of examiners and planning and building departments. The registration law came to Oregon only a decade or so later, along with the registration of architects, specifically 1919, but perhaps the writing was made visible on the wall, so to speak, by the new steel and concrete bank project. In any case, could Pugh have suspected that large-scale projects in his accustomed media and styles were perhaps no longer in the cards, leaving only private residences and small business buildings as potential projects?

And this leads, naturally, to the matter of money. It is impossible to say with any expectation of accuracy how Walter Pugh fared financially in this time of intense road building and street paving activity. By all appearances, he was doing quite well; he maintained several farms in the area. In February 1910, auctioneers sold a 200-acre farm belonging to Pugh on the Silverton Road, five miles northeast of Salem, and the livestock (including eight horses) and farm implements on it. A couple of weeks later, Pugh took an option on land in the vicinity of Luckiamute (on the Willamette River, between Independence and Albany) for $9,000. And in April 1910, he and Jessie bought 205 acres, also in Polk County, for $5,500.[238] Around that time, it was reported that he was driving (presumably in his new Oldsmobile) from his ranch near Rickreall (between Salem and Dallas). As has been previously noted, around the same time, he built a cottage on Waller Street and a bungalow on South Third Street, apparently as investments. He also apparently owned a rental on South Thirteenth Street.[239] At the end of 1911, according to a list of "improvements for 1911" in Salem, Pugh built a store at 700 North Capitol Street for $1,000, probably as a rental property.[240] At the end of February 1913, the Pughs were augmenting their Polk County ranch with another 35 acres for $2,788.[241] As late as May 1914, the Pughs bought a lot from one W.H. Darby, L1 B5 in the Yew Park addition, for $1,325.[242]

Judging from county clerk records for Marion County, Pugh had an earlier apparently flush period just as he was wrapping up his construction jobs for the Bureau of Indian Affairs. In 1902 and 1903, he and his wife had purchased significant acreage, mostly farmland without any structures.[243] Beginning in 1905, the Pugh family began spending vacation time in Newport, a fashionable destination for the gentry of Salem but also for people as far afield as Portland (no doubt, the easy rail connections from the valley helped make it popular.) On September 16, 1905, the *Capital Journal* reported, "Mrs. W.D. Pugh (with stepson Albert, still in school, and two-year old daughter, Katherine, no doubt) has returned from Newport, where she has been spending the summer months."[244] W.D. Pugh was reportedly visiting his family there on weekends for a couple of days at a time. In January 1906, Jessie Pugh bought a lot in Nye Beach.[245] We can safely assume that the contractor built a vacation cottage on it.

> *He had a fancy, expensive car that cost $3,000.00 when your mother was a very small child* [Mildred Irene, born in 1908; this must have been the Oldsmobile listed with his name in 1910], *a farm with registered stock—two modern homes and a huge barn. One house for the farmer and family who he paid by the month and one for us as a vacation home. We traveled by train with a fancy hunting dog called Stylish Fannie. He loved to hunt pheasants. He was late like your mother. I can remember them holding the train at the depot—the conductor walking up and down, looking at his watch while we arrived dog and all.*

It seems likely that the paving business seemed to promise significantly larger rewards than architecture at that particular time. An architect's fee was usually no more than 4 or 5 percent of a building's cost and could be paid out in segments over the often-significant period from first design to the completion of construction. Judging only from the number of competitors for paving jobs, it seems reasonable to conclude that they saw the possibility of significant returns—depending on their skill at predicting costs—more rapidly gained. And this brings us to the final chapter of W.D. Pugh's career as road builder.

"Maybe memories were painful to Dad," Pugh's daughter Katherine begins as she muses about why she and other family members (not including her mother, of course) knew nothing about his buildings. She had never heard about them until she came across an article about the Shelton-McMurphey house many years later; although she had visited Eugene with her parents more than once, she actually saw the home for the first time in 1995. She only knew about the "Whitespires" church in Albany in the 1970s, thanks to the campaign that was put in motion to save it.

So, what happened? Katherine saw the answer in his decision to become a contractor. "He was an artist not a businessman. That turned out to be a disaster," she wrote, not in reference to his work on the city streets of Salem from 1909 to 1913, but to a "huge contract to macadamize the highway between Monroe and Harrington, Washington. Rock crusher and all—a very expensive deal, and he had acquired a partner which [*sic*] did the book work and absconded with the money that should have paid the bills—leaving the operation in bankruptcy."

The bookkeeping partner in question was, of course, the aforementioned G.C. Arenz. Pugh partnered with several men on paving and road building jobs beginning in 1908. "Pugh and Herren" were reportedly finishing the grading and graveling of North Winter Street, from Market Street to the fairgrounds, in November 1908.[246] They got the contract to construct a new bridge across Mill Creek on South Commercial Street in March 1909 (at a bid of $4,649), a contract for improvements to Kearney Street in August 1909 and a contract for the South Water Street Bridge for a bid of $1,345.[247] After that, most of the bids and contracts were ascribed to Pugh alone, yet as late as April 1913, "W.D. Pugh and Mr. Herren" were in Stayton to place a bid with the city council for street paving.[248] It is not clear if the Mr. Herren who was partnered with Pugh was always the same person. Most likely, it was Levi M., the middle of the three sons of Noah Fowler Herren and Adeline Hall Herren; all three names show up in the newspapers' recordings of the work that was being done on Salem's streets in this period. The Herren family, like the Pughs, came to Oregon on the 1845 St. Joseph wagon train; the three sons, like Walter Pugh, were first-generation Oregonians.[249] It is perhaps no accident that all of Pugh's partners in both architecture and building were either from the same first Oregon-born generation of overland pioneers to Salem (Legg and Herrens), fellow graduates of Willamette (Gray and Legg) or both (Legg)—that is, until he teamed up with G.C. Arenz.

George Arenz, like Pugh, "an ardent believer in concrete pavement," was one member of a father-and-sons construction company that was incorporated in 1913.[250] Jacob Arenz, the patriarch, had been in the paving business for some time, and his son George continued to have his own company—even, on occasion, bidding for the same jobs as the parent Arenz company. Throughout this period, the Arenz Company bid on many of the same jobs as Pugh, and, as mentioned earlier in this chapter, they were involved, along with Pugh, in the "paving combine" that made news in May 1913.

On August 8, 1913, the *Statesman Journal* informed its readers: "SALEM MEN GET BIG JOB: G.C. Arenz and W.D. Pugh have been awarded a $40,000 paving contract at Monroe, Wash. They will leave for Monroe in four or five days."[251] This was the fateful job that Katherine refers to in her letter, to "macadamize the highway between Monroe and Harrington, Washington."

To be sure, this could only be an example of "macroscopic synecdoche," or using the whole to signify a part; $40,000 was a big job but not enough to pave the entire 266 miles between Monroe, near Seattle, to Harrington in eastern Washington, near Spokane. It was only enough to pave a part of it, although that may have been the most difficult part—from Monroe over the Cascade Mountains.

How long the Pugh and Arenz partnership lasted for work in Washington is not clear. An incidental remark in a Salem newspaper indicated that Mrs. Pugh (and presumably the Pughs' two young daughters, Katherine and Mildred Irene, born in September 1908) had joined Pugh and were staying in Everett. And the *Aberdeen Herald* reported, as late as May 22, 1914, that "work by Pugh & Arntz [*sic*] on a five-mile strip of grading and paving between Montesano and Satsop in southwestern Washington was progressing rapidly."[252]

At some point between late May and late October 1914, the Pugh and Arenz operation in Washington fell into arrears to the point that a series of lawsuits ensued, as reported in the court docket columns of the Aberdeen newspaper. These began with a suit for debt and attachment brought by Arenz's former partner in Salem paving jobs R.M. Hofer.[253] The attachment (*lis pendens*) was for property owned by Arenz in Hoquiam, Washington. (Aberdeen, Hoquiam and Montesano were all in Grays Harbor County.) There followed, in short order, a similar suit with the same attachment filed by W.D. Pugh against Arenz on November 3. At the same time, Pugh filed suit against Arenz for "accounting"; that is, presumably, for an accounting of their operations to date in Washington.[254]

Then, two months later, a default judgment "ordering that some property in this city [Salem] be sold, was rendered yesterday in the case of the Portland Railway, Light & Power Company against W.D. Pugh." The sums of the charges were $31.55, allegedly due for electric wiring and fixtures, and $13.60, assigned to the plaintiff by the Salem Fuel Company.[255] These were not large sums, even by 1915 standards, but the default judgment with an ordered sale of property suggests the existence of serious financial problems.

And, indeed, on March 10, 1915, the *Capital Journal* reported that a suit had been filed the day before in Marion County's circuit court by the Contractors Equipment Company of Washington for the collection of $300, with interest at 8 percent, from March 20, 1914, "upon a note said to be held against Walter D. Pugh and G.C. Arenz, doing business under the firm name of Pugh & Arenz, of this city, together with $50 attorney fees and a bill of $626.61 for goods and merchandise alleged to have been furnished them by the plaintiff between April 17 and September 22, 1914, no part of which, it is alleged, has ever been paid."[256]

Thus far, the story of the Washington venture of Pugh and Arenz is compatible with—if not a confirmation of—Katherine's story. Her father took on a big road job in Washington with a partner, who kept the books for the job or jobs and used the proceeds for some other purpose (to wit: the suit brought by Arenz's Salem partner, Hofer) than paying off job-related loans and bills to suppliers of equipment, goods and merchandise. According to the suit filed by the Contractors Equipment Company, nothing it furnished had ever been paid on an account going back to March 1914.

Again, the sums involved do not appear to add up to the financial disaster for Walter Pugh that Katherine describes: "He had to sell farms, stock, several properties and had nothing left but our house. That is when we came to 18th St. in 1920." It may be that Contractors Equipment had leased or simply rented road building equipment to Pugh & Arenz. Indeed, it is reasonable to conclude that the failure to service the debts involving the relatively modest sums of the suits mentioned previously suggest deeper financial difficulties. It seems likely that Pugh had accumulated significant debt, perhaps related to his real estate purchases of recent years, which he had no difficulty servicing while controlling his own business affairs in the Salem street paving years, and then had to take on more debt for materials and labor, which would normally be repaid from receipts on the completion of a job. It is not obvious that the Washington job (or jobs) were seriously underbid with the inevitable results for cash flow. Since Arenz was keeping the books, Pugh may have become aware of the situation (that construction job–related invoices and/or loans were not being paid or serviced) too late.

The deed records of Polk County shed some light on the situation. The 240 acres purchased by the Pughs for a total of $8,288 in April 1910 and February 1913 were sold by them at the end of September 1915 for $7,000, according to the warranty deed. From this sum, three encumbrances were deducted: two mortgages to W.H. Leeds for $500 and $2,500 and one mortgage for $4,000 in favor of the Monroe National Bank of Monroe, Washington, the total amounting to the sale price exactly.[257] The large mortgage that was held by the bank in Monroe does not necessarily belie serious cost calculations with the first Washington road job; a loan from a local bank to finance ongoing material and labor costs, repaid from receipts on the completion of a job, was nothing unusual. But that had obviously not been done.

And here, the plot thickens. Katherine writes at the end of her description of the Washington state road building debacle, "He had to sell farms, stock, several properties and had nothing left but our house. That is when we came to 18th St. in 1920." The house on Eighteenth Street was not built in 1920 but in 1921—a small detail—but Katherine passes over the more-than-five-year period that the family lived in Central Oregon. On October 6, 1915, Jessie H. Pugh purchased 158.47 acres of land near Sisters, Oregon, which was then still in Crook County but was soon to be Deschutes County, for $8,000. Three things about this sale draw attention. One is that the purchaser was Jessie Pugh alone; another is that she paid $50 an acre for land in the high desert country of central Oregon (granted, some of the Sisters land was irrigated, probably for grazing or alfalfa) after having sold land in the center of fertile Willamette Valley eleven days earlier for a little over $29 per acre. The third is that the purchasers of the land in the Willamette Valley and the sellers of the land in Central Oregon eleven days later were one and the same: Alvah and Caroline Prosser of Walla Walla, Washington.[258] Moreover, in April 1918, the Pughs "sold" the Sisters property to Jessie's father, Lemuel Hobson, for $1.[259] The conclusion seems fairly clear: the aim of these transactions for the Pughs was to settle with the mortgage holders, to shield some real property from seizure for other debts and to keep some amount of cash safe from creditors—how much probably depended on Prosser's differential valuation of the two properties.

The Pughs' purchase of the first 205-acre tract in Polk County for $5,500 in 1910 suggests that $29 per acre was probably close to the fair market value in that part of the Willamette Valley. At the end of February 1913, the Pughs had augmented their Polk County ranch with another 35 acres for $2,788.[260] Of course, we do not know how many or what kind of improvements had been made to the land before it was sold to the Prossers. This was almost certainly the farm with two houses that was described by Katherine. When Prosser, in turn, advertised the Polk County property, then known as Alva Prosser Ranch, for sale at auction in 1926, it was described as "choice 234-acre fruit ranch, 130 acres all improved, 104 acres timber and pasture, 17 acres in choice prunes, family orchard, grapes," including a description of the six-room house with a full basement and the four-room bungalow with modern conveniences, barns, a chicken house and so on.[261]

Alvah Asa Prosser (1851–1930), originally from Michigan, had been involved in land and timber deals in Oregon for some time. His residence at that time was in Walla Walla, Washington. It was probably after the 1926 sale of the Polk County ranch that Posser and his family moved to Portland, where Alvah died in 1930. No evidence could be found of the Prossers having been acquainted with the Pughs before this time. Prosser may have made a practice of being on the lookout for financial gain from troubled properties, perhaps with the specific goal of settling in the Willamette Valley. It is not known how the Prossers came by the Sisters property, but there is some indication that, in 1912, they were living in the Sisters area, possibly on the land that was later sold to Jessie Pugh "with appurtenances."[262] In any case, Prosser's participation in this deal goes far toward explaining why the Pughs moved from Salem to rural central Oregon in late 1915.

Meanwhile, the Arenz Construction Company had continued to bid for paving jobs in Salem but not without incident. At the end of December 1913, the city attorney stated that the company was to lose its bond for Market Street improvement for noncompliance.[263] Over the next few years, the company was bidding on jobs elsewhere in the valley and beyond, including state highway jobs west of Portland and as far as Astoria and the Siskiyou Mountain Grade in Jackson County. There was a big blow-up with the city of Astoria in January 1918. In order to fulfill eight contracts for municipal improvements in Astoria, the company had borrowed $60,000 from several banks, securing them with the contracts. The company then got into financial difficulties and failed to fulfill the contracts; the city intended to turn all the payments that were due over to the creditor banks.[264] In March 1920, the Multnomah County clerk was served a restraining order to prevent disbursement of $6,420.15 in his keeping, pending completion of a suit over that amount between the construction contractors Miller & Bauer and Jacob Arenz. This was done at the request of H.F. Bushong, the trustee of the bankrupt Arenz Construction Company. According to Bushong, the Arenz Construction Company had concealed from creditors $6,000 it owed Miller & Bauer for contracting work in Astoria in 1918. So, after the Arenz Construction Company had been discharged from bankruptcy, he sought its release so that it could be received by Arenz's creditors. Arenz claimed the money was due to him, personally. The judge ruled in favor of the creditors.[265]

In January 1921, George Arenz's debts finally caught up with him:

George C. Arenz, former local contractor and builder, filed an involuntary petition in bankruptcy Friday in the United States District Court. He gives his assets as $1,600 and liabilities as $4,577.59 [sic]. In addition to the liabilities, he lists 12 notes executed by the Arenz Construction Company of Portland, and delivered to the Astoria Savings Bank for $25,000, but *states he is unable to specify the amount due on each. "These notes are indorsed by Theodore Arenz and George C. Arenz."*

The assets named were due to Arenz from E.S. Small of Yakima for a carload of potatoes.[266]

Despite all of this, Arenz and his family's company continued to take paving jobs around western Oregon. The patriarch, Jacob, was solvent enough to hire a contractor to build a $3,500 residence in Portland.[267] In February 1922, George was laying pavement near Dayton.[268] Their father had died in 1924, but several of the Arenz sons, George, Theodore and Edward, continued with road and paving contracting. In April 1929, Arenz bid $142,612 for a 4.6-mile section of the Pacific Highway near Portland, which he won.[269] After 1929, George appears to have retired. His name crops up in the papers after that in connection with the "State Left-Handed Golf Association," of which he was an officer. He won the state southpaw golf championship in July 1930.[270] He died in 1938.

Theodore Arenz took on some sizeable Pacific Highway jobs up and down the state well into the 1930s. For example, he was low bidder on the Ashland undercrossing section of the Pacific Highway in Jackson County, as well as a section of the Willamette Highway near Oakridge.[271]

Through 1916 and into 1917, the Pughs' name appears on published lists of Salem property owners with property tax arrears. But W.D. Pugh never had to file for bankruptcy—at least a search of the federal district court archives revealed nothing, nor did a search of Salem newspapers, which closely monitored and reported on bankruptcy filings with the court.

THE PUGHS IN CENTRAL OREGON: 1915–20

How long the Pughs lived in the outback of Crook/Deschutes County on the former Prosser holding is not clear. In late August 1916, the *Capital Journal* noted, "Mrs. W.D. Pugh and daughters Catherine [*sic*] and Mildred, of Sisters, are in the city visiting the…parents of Mrs. Pugh."[272] By late 1917, at the latest, they had apparently moved to Bend, the new county seat.[273] Aside from occasional society page notes in the Bend paper ("Mr. and Mrs. W.D. Pugh and daughters, of Bend, spent Sunday in Sisters and Cloverdale visiting friends"), little is known about the Pughs' life in central Oregon.[274]

On August 11, 1918, the Salem papers carried the news that Albert W. Pugh, Walter's youngest son from his first marriage to Fannie Rhodes, had died of influenza at Fort McArthur, California, on Friday, November 1.[275] Albert Pugh was twenty-seven when he died of the Spanish flu at the San Pedro training camp, only two weeks after arriving from Portland with a draft contingent. As an unmarried man in the eighteen- to thirty-year-old age group, he was in category I-A of the draft, in accordance with the conscription law of June 5, 1917. Albert had lived in Salem his entire life— except for the last two to three years, which he spent in the South, perhaps Arkansas. (In any case, he had arrived from Arkansas for the funeral of his maternal grandfather, Allen Rhodes, in May 1915.) The event incidentally casts light on the impact of America's 1917 entry into World War I on life in Oregon. The notice of his death included information about his siblings from Walter Pugh's first marriage: his brother Allen was working in the Portland shipyards, and his sister Inez was in Newport News, Virginia, where her husband, Dr. E.E. Cable, was in the service, for which he, as a married man, had probably volunteered.[276]

Evidence of architectural or contracting activity by Walter Pugh in Central Oregon is scant. Apparently, he did design another bank building in Redmond in 1919. An article in the *Bend Bulletin* on July 26, 1919, announced that the First National Bank of Redmond was to have a new building, at 404 Southwest Fourth Street, "a combination of brick and stone, and with fixtures, [it] will cost about $25,000. Features of the building will be a restroom for ladies and a private room for meetings. W.D. Pugh and R.A. Nelson of Bend have the contract for the building."[277] The last sentence suggests that Pugh and Nelson were the building contractors. However, the "Oregon Inventory of Historic Properties' Historic Resource Survey Form" leaves the "architect" rubric blank and identifies the "builder" as Ole Olson, a well-known building contractor of the region (as do other sources).[278] The fifty-foot-tall, rectangular, two-story corner building, variously described in the inventory as "modern" or "colonial," could very well be fitted into the Pugh bank canon: buff brick with a stone apron, decorative brick cornice and four large, in this case, Egyptian-style columns punctuating the inset entrance façade on Fourth Street.

On August 14, 1919, we learn from the Bend paper, "Miss Catherine [*sic*] Pugh" left for Salem to attend Salem High School.[279] There is no similar report for the following year, so perhaps Katherine was accurate in writing that the family returned to Salem in 1920. In any case, the reentry of W.D. Pugh into the newspaper reports on paving and road construction affairs around Salem occurs for the first time, perhaps, in an article from August 21, 1921. The article reports a lawsuit that was brought by the city

First National Bank of Redmond (1919). *Courtesy of the Oregon Inventory of Historic Properties, Historic Resource Survey form, local I.D. no. 57, county: Deschutes, June 23, 1997.*

of Dallas for one M.H. Pangra against Walter D. Pugh and Henry Sauer for $700 worth of sand and gravel that had been used while the defendants were constructing sidewalks for the city of Dallas on a contract from 1920. The defendants filed a demurrer, asserting there were "insufficient facts to constitute a cause of action." The case was settled a month later with the payment of the contested sum without interest.[280]

Then, in short order, Pugh and Sauer sued the city of Dallas for a collection of $1,219.68, an uncollected balance of the total of $17,078 for sidewalk construction, which the city set aside—2 percent—as a guarantee of acceptable condition. The city's position that "not all...had proven satisfactory" was not justified, the plaintiffs argued, because the city had removed barricades along some streets too early, resulting in a bad surface. The case ended in a hung jury.[281]

The Pugh & Sauer sidewalk construction venture came to an end on or before May 16, 1922, the day of Sauer's death at the age of fifty-four.[282] Shortly thereafter, and obviously in the works for some time before Sauer's death, W.D. Pugh, in partnership with S.A. Hughes, won a $47,100 contract to build a new Methodist Old People's Home on Center Street in Salem. This included the building, complete with plumbing and heating, all ready to move in, and it was to be completed in six months. The building was to include two full stories, an attic and a basement, eventually for sixty guests. "It will be one of the most complete plants of its kind anywhere. There are no stairways, but long, inclined runways, on a one-to-seven-grade….Every facility for giving comfort, safety, pleasure, to the guests is to be provided."[283]

That Pugh should reenter the competition for building contracts in Salem with such a plum job was more than likely helped by the persons with whom he was associated in the enterprise. S.A. Hughes was a prominent figure in Salem, a three-term member of the state legislature, representing Marion County before 1920 and later, and a perennial member of the city council (alderman for the second ward). A bricklayer by trade, he had gone on to have a career in contracting—a recent job he'd had was the construction of a heating plant at the Chemawa Indian School—and other business ("a heavy taxpayer," as one article put it). In at least two of these capacities, he must have had previous dealings with Walter Pugh and possibly in other respects as well: both were passionate pheasant hunters, and both were Democrats. He also must have been well acquainted with Walter's younger brother David W. Pugh, who had been Salem's fire chief for many years.

And the architect for the building was none other than Pugh's former partner, Fred A. Legge (a spelling of his name that he adopted in the meantime), who had moved his office back to Salem in 1916.[284]

There is no indication that Pugh had any other building contracts worthy of note by the newspapers over the next few years. He ran an advertisement under the "Contractors-Building" rubric for a time in 1924.[285] Then, in June 1925, an article in the *Statesman Journal* revealed, "Walter Pugh, Salem architect" had provided the plans for "the Salem Branch of the Ryan Fruit Company's…new home. Building erected and equipped especially for this line of business, making everything up to date and ship-shape for carrying on the operations here.…It is one of the best equipped buildings in this respect in the valley." The building's contractor was David W. Pugh.[286] The fact that Walter had not taken advantage of the grandfather clause under the 1919 state law requiring the registration of architects did not, apparently, prevent the issuance of the building permit for that job.

The new regime, with planning departments and building inspections, was already in operation when David Pugh, the contractor, was reportedly applying for building permits for commercial buildings in 1926 and as late as 1931. After 1925, the only building permits issued to Walter Pugh were for construction of a garage at his property, 451 [actually 441] North Eighteenth Street, in 1927 and for reroofing it in 1940.[287]

In May 1928, P.L. Frazier and W.D. Pugh were awarded a county contract to erect two concrete culverts on county market roads for $2,690.50 and $1,557.00, respectively.[288] Frazier, a graduate of Willamette Law School, was a contractor specializing in concrete, especially bridge work, at that time.[289]

By the late 1920s, even before the stock market crash in the autumn of 1929, it appears that construction activity in Salem had decreased considerably. At any rate, architects and contractors could be seen competing for salaried government jobs. In October 1928, the city of Salem, anticipating the adoption of a building code (passed by the city council on December 17), advertised for the position of city building inspector, "a coveted plum from now henceforth."[290] Both W.D. Pugh and Fred A. Legge applied, unsuccessfully, for the job. In 1933, David W. Pugh was serving as chairman of the city planning and zoning commission. In 1934, P.L. Frazier was running for both county judge and (on the Democratic ticket) county commissioner.[291]

In June 1932, the *Statesman Journal* reported, "Mr. and Mrs. W.D. Pugh, who have been for some time in Lewiston, Idaho, where Mr. Pugh is employed, are making their headquarters here while on vacation. They are now travelling in eastern Oregon, accompanied by their son-in-law and daughter, Mr. and Mrs. Clarence Emmons."[292] The nature and exact duration of this second Pugh displacement eastward could not be determined, nor could the nature of the employment, but it was possibly for a logging or lumber concern. In any case, the Pughs kept their North Eighteenth Street houses and probably a vacation cottage in Newport, Nye Beach, and by the summer of 1936, at the latest, they were back in western Oregon. On July 28, the *Statesman Journal* reported:

> *Mrs. Walter D. Pugh of Salem, who has been living in Newport for several months, is convalescing at her home at 441 North 18th Street following an automobile accident which occurred on the Salmon River cutoff, near Grande Ronde last Thursday....Riding with Mrs. Pugh was Nancy Lea Montgomery [her granddaughter]...who received a slight scalp wound. Mrs. Pugh suffered an injury to a vertebra. She expects to return to Newport, where Mr. Pugh is constructing a building, after a few days rest here.[293]*

This barely identified project may have been W.D. Pugh's last job as a building contractor. The mention of his name in the Salem papers occurs rarely after this incident.

In a brief notice in the same Salem paper, on September 18, 1937, the Pughs are identified as residents of Monroe, Oregon: "Mr. and Mrs. Walter D. Pugh, of Monroe, Oregon, parents of Mrs. Emmons, cared for David and Terry during the absence of Mr. and Mrs. Emmons [for a convention of the "Twenty-Thirty Club" in Reno]."[294] The Pughs are known to have spent time somewhat later in a small house (without indoor plumbing) in the country, near Monroe. Perhaps they were renting out the Salem house at this time.

In 1942, the Pughs' fortieth wedding anniversary was remarked on in the *Statesman Journal*: "Mr. and Mrs. Walter D. Pugh celebrated their 40th wedding anniversary with their children Wednesday night, when the group went to Portland for dinner. The couple have lived in Salem since their marriage."[295] On April 5, 1943, the *Capital Journal* marked architect Walter D. Pugh's eightieth birthday by listing some of his best-known works in Salem, beginning with the city hall and ending with the old Salem High School building. It concluded: "There were numerous others."[296]

And finally, "WALTER PUGH, PIONEER STATE ARCHITECT, DIES.

> *Walter David Pugh, pioneer…Salem resident and well-known Oregon architect, died Friday at his…residence, 441 N. 18th St., after a short illness.*
>
> *Many of Salem's older buildings and houses were designed by Pugh, among…them being the city hall, the dome of the old state capitol building, as well as…many residences. As state architect under Gov. Pennoyer, Pugh designed…many state institution buildings. Kidder Hall at Oregon State College, halls at…Chemawa Indian School, and buildings for the Indian reservation at Phoenix, Ariz., were also part of Pugh's work.*
>
> *Surviving are the widow, Mrs. Jessie H. Pugh; three daughters, Mrs. Inez E. Cable, Portland, and Mrs. Katherine Montgomery and Mrs. Mildred Emmons, both of Salem; a son, Allen E. Pugh, Hermiston, Ore; a brother, Dave W. Pugh, Salem; nine grandchildren and two great-grandchildren.*[297]

CONCLUSION

Walter Pugh, Pioneer State Architect" was, indeed, the first "pioneer" state architect, but he was not, strictly speaking, a pioneer architect. That was his father, David Hall Pugh, who had walked across the plains as a young boy. Walter Pugh was a pioneer in this sense: he was the first Oregon-born and educated architect to make a significant contribution to Oregon's built landscape. All of his professional contemporaries (and competitors) who were working in Oregon in the quarter century between 1885 and 1910, were born and mostly educated elsewhere, especially on the East Coast. One partial exception was Fred A. Legg, who was only three years Pugh's junior and, like Pugh, the Willamette-educated son of a pioneer, but he entered the profession much later than Pugh, making his debut near the end of Pugh's marathon stretch as architect—taking up, as it were, the architect's torch during their four-year partnership between 1905 and 1909.

In several ways, Pugh's story as an architect and as a builder was a matter of being in the right place at the right time. He entered the architectural profession in Salem when extensive building of state institutions there was getting underway as a result of the constitutionally mandated moving of these institutions from Portland to the capital city (the state prison, the insane asylum, et cetera). This was also a time of rapid population growth that set in when the Willamette Valley got hooked up to rail networks: the population of Oregon rose from 90,000 on the eve of the opening of the valley to continental rail traffic in 1871 to 413,000 by 1900, most of it in the Willamette Valley. There was continuous expansion of the state penitentiary and the state insane asylum from the mid-1880s to the 1900s, through the years of the Pugh & Legg partnership. As late as mid-1907, the partnership was calling for bids on a large wing of the asylum. And then, the momentum of state institution building was continued in 1908, following the decision to create a "State Institution for the Feeble-Minded and Epileptic." This institution was populated, at first, by transfers from the insane asylum, which Pugh was deeply involved with, first as an architect and then as building contractor. This project was just getting underway when Pugh & Legg took on the design for the buildings of the Oregon School of Deaf Mutes when its board of trustees decided to move it from the countryside to Salem.

In the same context of population growth and the development of state and public institutions in the still-young state of Oregon, Pugh, early on, made his mark with the rise of the state system of higher education, especially at the new agricultural college in Corvallis, where his design of Benton Hall (1887) established his reputation as an important figure in Oregon architecture. Other buildings on the campus of the future Oregon State College (eventually Oregon State University) followed. The much smaller Pugh "footprint" at the University of Oregon—and his smaller footprint as a building contractor—is explainable, in part, by the university's later start and enduring financial difficulties in the late nineteenth century. At the same time, the agricultural college, as a land-grant institution, with its practical science and technology focus, especially as applied to agriculture, more readily attracted state and federal funding.

The development of primary and secondary education called for the design of numerous buildings. Pugh was on hand when the demand for high school education as a constituent part of public education came to the foreground around the turn of the century. He designed both Salem's and Eugene's first high schools. His work throughout the heavily vested almost twenty years of his architectural career is punctuated by his designs for school buildings all around the central Willamette Valley.

The same process of rapid population growth and urban development afforded orders for city halls. Pugh designed the city halls of both Salem and Corvallis. One might add here the design of the Crook County Courthouse as the product of intercity competition for—or defense of—its county seat status.

Since the time of the gold rush, the Willamette Valley had been a significant source of wheat and lumber, exportable by the river-to-sea system (Hawaii was a major destination of valley wheat production early on), and this was accelerated by the arrival of railroad connections to the east. By the 1870s and 1880s, not only Portland, but Salem and even smaller towns had significant groups, if not classes, of merchants-become-capitalists who were seeking to put their wealth to work building banks and commercial buildings.[298] Pugh was designing buildings for these clients, especially in— but by no means limited to—Salem, virtually from the time he appeared on the scene. His mark on the urban landscape of Salem was particularly evident in the fire prevention–inspired building boom of the late 1880s. But commercial buildings remained significant parts of his work well into the first decade of the twentieth century.

The law in 1891 that required the federal government to provide education for Native peoples provided yet more opportunities for Walter Pugh—this time, as building contractor. That part of his career, which started in 1897 with some contract work at the Warm Springs Reservation, led to a rapid series of building projects for the Bureau of Indian Affairs, both on reservations (Warm Springs, Siletz, Fort Mohave, et cetera) and, especially, off reservations (Phoenix, Chemawa, et cetera). In fact, these projects constituted the bulk of his activity as a building contractor and largely occupied his time in the six years between 1897 and 1902. There were, of course, other building contracts, both within that period (McClure Hall, 1899) and later (Fairview Home, 1909; Methodist Old People's Home, 1922).

Not to be forgotten are the numerous private homes, at least thirty, that he designed between 1887 and 1908. Most of these projects were done in Salem or the surrounding area; at least three were done elsewhere, including the Shelton-McMurphey house in Eugene, at the beginning of his architectural career, and two were done in Portland near the end of his career. The Portland houses were probably contracted for and quite likely designed by Fred Legg during their partnership. The same may be true of at least some of the Salem houses he designed in 1907 and 1908.

It should be noted that neither Pugh nor Legg, before or during their maintenance of an office in Portland, ever broke into the Portland high-end residence market in a significant way. A hub of northwest shipping and commerce and with a vastly larger population than any other city in Oregon, Portland had its own established architectural firms well before the appearance of Pugh or Legg on the scene. True, the firm had several commercial buildings in Portland to its credit in the years between 1906 and 1909, and Legg worked out of his Portland office for several years before closing it and returning to Salem after 1915.[299] However, it must be said that the least satisfying representation of Pugh's legacy is in the architecture of private residences. Aside from the well-known Shelton-McMurphey mansion in Eugene, dating back to 1887, and the Duniway house on State Street in Salem, which he built twenty-one years later, none of these buildings appear to have survived long enough to have been nominated for listing in the National Register of Historic Places, nor do photographic images of them appear to be available online (Building Oregon, Oregon Historical Photograph Collections).[300]

Finally, Pugh's work as a paving and road building contractor was made possible by his being present, willing and able at the advent of the automobile age. Pugh paved a considerable number of Salem's streets before setting out on his ultimately ill-fated road building enterprise with G.C. Arenz in Washington.

EPILOGUE

In the introduction of this book, I explained that the only way to know more about my grandfather, whom I, as a young boy, knew only as an old man, was to investigate what he did. Where did he learn to be an architect in Salem, Oregon, in the 1880s? He had designed—or was it built—the city hall in Salem, but what else did he design? Why did no one in the family know about the many other Pugh projects or at least ever talk about what they knew? When did he stop working as an architect? Why did he and his family live for some time in central Oregon?

The resulting book, also noted in the introduction, is a kind of hybrid: neither a straightforward study of a regional expression of architectural trends in the United States and Europe of the late nineteenth century nor a conventional biography.

What it has produced is documentation of a remarkable twenty-odd-year career of architectural activity, most of it individual activity—he was his own draftsman most of the time, apparently—that had been undocumented and largely unknown. If much about the architectural legacy of Walter Pugh was largely unknown, his career as a builder was completely unknown. I am satisfied that, in the end, the exploration of both areas of his activity produced significant knowledge about his personal life and circumstances that would have otherwise remained quite obscure.

In the absence of personal archives, building department records (for most of the years of W.D. Pugh's activity), memoirs and diaries, an inquiry such as this would have been practically impossible without the digitization, with keyword searching capability, of local newspapers. In the years of Walter Pugh's active career, local newspapers recorded all sorts of things that were going on locally and employed reporters to follow them. They reported on things that would be difficult to imagine one reporting on today: not only the police beat, court docket, fires and social events, but also the comings and goings on the train, listings of persons checking in (and out) of the local hotels, family reunions with a recitation of all persons present and, of course, business affairs, play-by-play accounts of city council meetings and building activities of all sorts.

The reliance here on the local press, as a glance at the endnotes will show, certainly has its limits. Reporters did commit errors of fact; no doubt, certain kinds of behavior by influential citizens went unreported, as did many other things deemed of little interest to the general public at the time and so on. A considerable amount of information was obtained with the help of the staff members of numerous institutions—from the Oregon State Archives; county clerks' records; the Oregon State Library; Salem Public Library; the archives of Oregon State University and Willamette University, state, county and city historical societies; online data and image collections; and more.

However, without my reliance on the newspapers of the day, much that has been learned for this story would not have been possible. I would like to think this exercise might serve as an example of the potential of the study of history "at ground level."

And finally, on the technology front, the collection of material for this study, both printed and, especially, visual, considering its subject's profession, would have been impossible without the humble screenshot.

LISTS OF BUILDINGS DESIGNED OR BUILT BY W.D. PUGH IN CHRONOLOGICAL ORDER

A Note to the Reader

The architectural and contracting projects of W.D. Pugh are recorded together in three lists, in keeping with the historical-biographical approach of the book as a whole.

The first lists municipal, county, state and federal institutions and buildings that are used by the public for noncommercial purposes, such as theaters, fraternal organizations and churches. The second lists banks and residences that were built as investments (rental/leasing) as well as stores, offices, livery stables, processing plants and the like. The third lists private residences.

The dates preceding most architecture entries are the dates of the newspaper announcements that solicited contractors' bids for a given building. For contracting jobs, they are usually the dates on which the winning bids were reported. Projects lacking such reports are given without a month or day.

In all three categories, all of the architectural projects were signed off by W.D. Pugh alone or in partnership (Pugh & Legg, for example). In a few cases, as discussed in the text, the authorship of one or the other partner alone is clear. In others, it is not, and the assumption there is that Pugh, as senior partner, was significantly involved in the firm's projects and, therefore, merits authorship.

LIST OF PUBLIC BUILDINGS DESIGNED OR BUILT IN CHRONOLOGICAL ORDER

Key: **d**—designed; **s**—supervised construction; **b**—built.

1885

August 28. Additional shops on Oregon State Penitentiary ground. Plans and specs at the office of Boothby & Pugh, architects, in Salem, Oregon.

1887

August 19. State Agricultural College building (administration building and Benton Hall), Corvallis, Oregon (d, s) ($20,000).

1888

March 23. New brick building at the state penitentiary in Salem, Oregon (d) ($6,000 appropriation).

May 18. Dallas hotel opposite Dallas City Hall, three stories (d), Dallas, Oregon ($7,000).

1890

May 8. Eight-room schoolhouse, Marion County School District, no. 24 (d).

1891

March 26. United Presbyterian Church (Whitespires), Albany, Oregon (d) ($15,000).

June 13. State Agricultural College, student dormitory (Cauthorn Hall, Kidder Hall, Fairbanks Hall), Corvallis, Oregon (d).

August 21. State Agricultural College, chemical laboratory, Corvallis, Oregon (d).

August 21. City hall, three stories, Corvallis, Oregon (d).

1892

January 29. New capitol dome, Salem, Oregon (s).

March 4. Park school, Salem, Oregon (d).

May 26. School building, District 54 (Clymer), Salem, Oregon (d).

1893

State Agricultural College, mechanical hall, Corvallis, Oregon (d).

May 12. Post office building, seventy-five by one hundred feet, two stories, Albany, Oregon (d).

1894

State Agricultural College, horticulture building, Corvallis, Oregon (d).

January 21. IOOF building, wooden, two stories, forty-two by fifty-four feet, Hubbard, Oregon (d).

June 11. New city hall, Salem, Oregon (d, s) ($5,4675; architect's fee of 4 percent or $2,187).

1896

November 23. Warm Springs Indian Agency, school buildings, Jefferson County, Oregon (b).

1897

April 5. New post office, 304 Commercial Street, Salem, Oregon (d).

1898

March 25. U.S. Indian Training School in Phoenix, Arizona; contract for erection of five new buildings (b, with Chas. A. Gray) (approximately $40,000).

1899

June 24. Fort Mohave Indian School, Arizona, dormitory (b).

August 5. University of Oregon, contract for erecting new university science building (McClure Hall), Eugene, Oregon (b, with Chas. A. Gray).

1900

IOOF (opera house, Grand Theater), Salem, Oregon (d).

May 22. Insane asylum, closed cottage, Salem, Oregon (d, s, Pugh & Gray).

June 4. State penitentiary, new wing, et cetera, Salem, Oregon (d, Pugh & Gray).

1901

March 29. State Soldiers' Home, one barracks building and an addition to the then-present hospital, Roseburg, Oregon (d).

October 1. Salem Indian School (Chemawa), brick dormitory ($19,386), brick industrial building ($5,040), brick laundry ($3,494), Salem/ Chemawa (b, with Fremont Van Patten).

1903

April 15. New high school building, stone and brick (approximately $25,000) (later, city hall), Eugene, Oregon (d).

April 18. Plans for "a grand arch at the state fairgrounds," Salem, Oregon (d).

May 15. Insane asylum, building contract for "closed cottage" and extension of dining hall ($19,350), Salem, Oregon (d).

July 23. School building, construction of a one-story building, Marion County, Oregon (d).

1904

First Congregational Church, corner of Liberty and Center Streets, Salem, Oregon (d, Pugh & Carey).

1905

January 24. New high school, 171 by 80 feet ($50,000), Salem, Oregon (d, s).

April 7. State fairgrounds, construction of buildings, et cetera, that were to be "extensive and of a permanent character," to include: an addition to the banquet hall, roofed-over floral garden, an addition to the south end of the pavilion, a seventy-foot addition to the north end of the grandstand, decomposed granite sidewalks, a sewer system, in Salem, Oregon (around $15,000) (d).

July 19. Willamette University, medical college building ($15,000) (d, Pugh & Legg).

1906

June 2. Crook County Courthouse, Prineville, Oregon (d).

1907

January 21. School, two-story, brick, Carlton, Oregon (d) (Pugh & Legg).

February 11. North St. Johns School, ninety-one by sixty-six feet, two stories, concrete basement, frame, Portland, Oregon (d) (Pugh & Legg)

March 20. Eastern extension of north wing, insane asylum, Salem (d; s)

May 14. Insane asylum, construct and complete brick asylum wing with plumbing, hot water, et cetera, (low bid: $81,895), Salem, Oregon (d) (Pugh & Legg).

December 25. St. Johns School, two stories, frame, sixty-five by ninety feet, Portland, Oregon (d) (Pugh & Legg).

1908

February 26. State Institution for the Feeble-Minded, administration building, H shape, 40 by 60 feet, 36 by 104 feet, 26 by 36 feet, two stories, frame Colonial style with four columns, Salem, Oregon (d).

February 26. State Institution for the Feeble Minded, laundry, brick, one story, thirty by thirty-six feet, Salem, Oregon (d).

February 26. Barn, two stories; frame horse and cow barn, 38 by 120 feet; carriage room; two silos; stables; et cetera, Salem, Oregon (d).

February 26. Boiler house, brick, one story, thirty by thirty-six feet, Salem, Oregon (d).

March 26. Crook County Courthouse, Prineville, Oregon (d) (first plans submitted on June 2, 1906).

May 19. Liberty School (d).

1909

April 16. Oregon School for the Deaf (d, Pugh & Legg).

June 12. State Institution for Feeble-Minded, building contract for two dormitories, frame with brick basement, 43 by 124 feet ($29,442), Salem, Oregon (b).

1922

June 9. New Methodist Old People's Home, Sixteenth and Center Streets, Salem, Oregon (b, Pugh & Hughes).

LIST OF COMMERCIAL/BUSINESS BUILDINGS IN CHRONOLOGICAL ORDER

Key: (**d**—designed; **s**—supervised **b**—built by)

1887

April 23. Dr. Josephi, sanitorium, East Portland, Oregon (d) ($7,000–$10,000).

1888

March 23. Two-story building just north of the State Insurance Company's building, on the corner of Commercial and Chemeketa Streets, Salem, Oregon (d).

March 23. Four cottages for John Q. Wilson, on Center Street between Commercial and Liberty Streets; they are all alike and rentals, in Salem, Oregon (d) ($1,100 each).

May 5. Three-story office building for State Insurance Company, Salem, Oregon (d).

May 18. New three-story hotel, modern design, one hundred guests; work on foundation was underway, Dallas, Oregon (d).

1889

Bush-Breyman Block, 135–141–147 Commercial Street, Northeast, Salem, Oregon (d).

Bush and Brey Block and Annex, 179–195–197 Commercial Street Northeast, Salem, Oregon (d) ($6,000).

Eldridge Block, three stories, east side of Commercial Street, from R.M. Wade North to Chemeketa Streets, Salem, Oregon (d).

Thos. Kay Woolen Mill Co. building, 110 by 55 feet, three stories, was available to bidders at the office of Walter Pugh, Salem, Oregon (d).

1891

Independence National Bank, Independence, Oregon (d).

1892

Dr. T.L. Golden, double tenement house on Liberty Street, on a vacant lot north of Dr. Golden's residence, Salem, Oregon (d).

June 3. A. Bush, a new brick building adjoining Ladd & Bush Bank, Salem, Oregon (d).

July 2. Thomas Holman, a new brick building, fifty by one hundred feet, just south of his present building on State Street. The new building was constructed specially for an electric light and power station, Salem, Oregon (d).

1893

July 1. Thomas Burrows, brick, a Commercial Street continuation of the Paul Oberheim Block, with same style front, Salem, Oregon (d).

1894

March 27. Four one-story buildings, ninety-one-by-twenty-one-foot frontage, replacing burned block, Woodburn, Oregon (d).

1895

December 21. Thos. Kay Woolen Mill, new woolen mill plans completed, Salem, Oregon (d).

1901

August 11. Commercial building between Waters Cigar Store and Eckerlen Block (145–147 Northeast Liberty Street), two-story brick, thirty by ninety feet, Salem, Oregon (d).

1902

May 1. E.S. Lamport, brick livery stable, Salem, Oregon (d).

May 15. Maurice Klinger, two-story brick business block, Salem, Oregon (d).

June 29. Douglas County Bank, two-story brick, corner of Oak and Jackson Streets, Roseburg, Oregon (d).

July 9. August Schreiber, two-story brick building with basement, Salem, Oregon (d).

December 16. New opera house, next to Day & Henderson Block on Willamette Street, Eugene, Oregon (d, s).

1903

February 6. New livery stable for John A. Simpson, just south of W.C. Tillson & Co., feed store, 65 by 165 feet, two stories, brick, Salem, Oregon (d).

1904

February 15. E.S. Lamport, new building at 289 Commercial Street, Salem, Oregon (d).

1905

April 28. D.F. Wagner, two-story block, 387 Court Street, next to the Steusloff Bros. building (399 Court Street), Salem, Oregon (d).

July 9. Two-story brick building on corner of Liberty and State Streets for Louis Vierani's heirs, Salem, Oregon (d).

1906

August 25. Benton County National Bank, Corvallis, Oregon (d, Pugh & Legg).

November 22. W. Yanke livery stable, two stories, brick and basement, Salem, Oregon (d) (Pugh & Legg).

November 23. Store building on Southeast Sixth Avenue, at or near Southeast Hawthorne Street, Portland, Oregon (d) (Pugh & Legg).

1907

January 4. James Olson, hotel, Southeast Grand Street, at or near Southeast Hawthorne Boulevard, Portland, Oregon (d) (Pugh & Legg).

January 8. Mixed multi-residence and store, Portland, Oregon (d) (Pugh & Legg).

January 29. W.H. Lang, hotel, Southwest Front Avenue, at or near Southwest Harrison Street, Portland, Oregon (d) (Pugh & Legg).

May 25. H. Goldstein building, 405 Southwest First Street, at the corner of Southwest First Avenue, commercial stores ($6,000), Portland, Oregon (d) (Pugh & Legg).

June 26. Mrs. T. Halversen, residences/apartments, two-story frame flats, Southeast Main Street, between Southeast Thirteenth and Southeast Fourteenth Avenues ($5,000), Portland, Oregon (d) (Pugh & Legg).

December 23. East Portland Masonic Temple, Southeast Eighth Avenue, at the southwest corner of East Burnside Street. Mixed stores and other purposes, two stories, brick and terra-cotta, basement, four stores, one hundred by sixty-five feet, Portland, Oregon (d) (Pugh & Legg).

1908

May 17. W.D. Pugh, two new houses on Waller Street, between Twelfth and Thirteenth Avenues ($1,500 each), rentals, Salem, Oregon (d).

June 12. United States National Bank of Salem, under construction at the corner of State and Commercial Streets. Steel, stone and brick (Pugh & Legg) ($100,000).

December 27. Messrs. Brownstein & Son, one-story concrete garage and stable, Salem, Oregon (d, Pugh & Legg).

1910

January 1. D.W. Pugh, cottage ($1,600) on Waller Street; bungalow at 969 South Thirteenth Avenue ($1,800), Salem, Oregon (d, s, b).

1911

December 30. W.D. Pugh, store building, 700 North Capitol Street ($1,000), Salem, Oregon (d, b).

1919

July 26. New Redmond Bank building contract ($25,000), Redmond, Oregon (d, W.D. Pugh and R.A. Nelson of Bend).

1925

June 25. Ryan Fruit Co., Salem branch, operations (building contractor: David W. Pugh), Salem, Oregon (d).

List of Private Residences in Chronological Order

Key: (**d**—designed; **s**—supervised construction; **b**—built)

1886

May 1. "A fine cottage on Chemeketa between Twelfth and Capitol Streets," (for himself) (d, b).

1887

March 20. A.N. Gilbert residence, Chemeketa and Liberty Streets, Salem, Oregon (d) ($4,000).

April 21. New wing of the insane asylum (state hospital), Salem, Oregon (d, s).

April 29. H.H. Smith residence, State and Tenth Streets, two stories, Salem, Oregon (d) ($1,800).

Shelton-McMurphey-Johnson House, Eugene, Oregon ($8,000) (d).

1892

February 19. George Pearce residence on Winter Street, Salem, Oregon (d).

February 27. E.S. Lamport, two-story residence, Salem, Oregon (d) (replaced in 1929).

March 23. William Feldt, two frame cottages, Salem, Oregon (d).

September 12. New barn, eighty by thirty-two feet, Salem, Oregon (d).

1893

February 22. A.J. Chatwin's new house, Salem, Oregon (d).

May 25. John Newsome's cottage in south Salem, frame structure, Salem, Oregon (d) (about $1,000).

April 14. Thomas Sims, two-story house and basement, East State Street, Salem, Oregon (d) ($4,000).

June 16. Feeley residence, in the vicinity of East School, Salem, Oregon (d) ($1,500–$1,800).

October 26. E.Y. Lansing, two stories, stone foundation, near Salem, Oregon (d) ($3,300–$4,000).

1894

July 12. Sorgent McCabe residence, Salem, Oregon (d) (around $2,000).

1895

March 31. Mrs. A.W. Demitt, new residence North Winter Street, in Boise's addition, Salem, Oregon (d) ($845–$1,175).

August 9. George Townsend of Perrydale, new farm and residence (d).

1898

February 1. Building of a small cottage, Salem, Oregon (d).

1900

S. Friedman, cottage, at the corner of Church and Center Streets, Salem, Oregon (d).

1905

January 1. W.D. Pugh's new home, a cottage at the northwest corner of Winter and Union Streets, Salem, Oregon (d, b).

1906

November 3. Mrs. Louise Fritz's house, single family, two-story frame, Sunnyside, Portland, Oregon (d, Pugh & Legg) ($2,500).

1907

April 24. Z. Riggs house, a new single-family residence, Salem, Oregon (d) (Pugh & Legg).

April 24. Mayor Rodgers's house, single-family residence, Salem, Oregon (d) (Pugh & Legg).

June 12. Mrs. F.P. Waring's house, on Northeast Weidler Street, between Northeast Seventeenth and Northeast Eighteenth Avenues, single-family residence, frame, Portland, Oregon (d) (Pugh & Legg) ($4,750).

1908

John Bayne's house, single-family residence, Salem, Oregon (d) (Pugh & Legg) ($2,500).

April 8. William Brown's house, alterations and additions, Salem, Oregon (d) (Pugh & Legg) ($3,500)

April 8. Willis S. Duniway's house, new single-family residence, Salem, Oregon, (d) new (Pugh & Legg) ($4,000).

April 8. Mrs. S.C. Dyer's house, new single-family residence, Salem, Oregon (d) (Pugh & Legg) ($3,000).

April 8. Ray L. Farmer's house, single-family residence at the corner of Thirteenth Avenue and Center Street, the south side of Center Street, Salem, Oregon (d) (Pugh & Legg) ($3,500).

April 8. C.H. Hinges's house, new single-family residence, Salem, Oregon (d) (Pugh & Legg) ($2,500).

1921–1924

Pugh residence, frame duplex, 441 North Eighteenth Street, Salem, Oregon (d, b).

Possible Pugh rental, frame, stucco, next door to 435 North Eighteenth Street, Salem, Oregon (d, b).

1927

May 12. W.D. Pugh issued permit to build a $409 garage at 451 [*sic*] North Eighteenth Street, Salem, Oregon (d, b).

1940

Walter Pugh was issued a permit to reroof the garage at 442 North Eighteenth Street ($40).

LETTER OF KATHERINE PUGH
SCHWABAUER, 1995

Salem, OR
September 30, 1995

Dear Terry,

I was pleased to hear from you, and I am sorry my explanation of the Workmans was not clear. Their story intrigued me—coming into the wilderness to start a new life in southern Oregon when life was primitive, indeed. They were no one we knew but, nevertheless, were real people who loved the country and its lifestyle—or at least came to love it.

Saturday, I went to Eugene to visit Ramona and to salvage the lawn I paid for! I sat on the front lawn from a few minutes after 7:00 a.m. until 3:30 p.m. digging weeds and putting weed killer in the holes. I had breakfast on the lawn and lunch on the back porch. I dug 4 bushels (construction size buckets that material comes in), and she helped me with the last two, which made 6 altogether—and that was without a pottie stop, too? Then I edged the whole thing with hand clippers on my knees. How is that for 92+. One might say an exhibition of "no sense at all?"

The highlight of that trip was Ramona took me to see and visit the "Castle on the Hill" in Eugene. How could I live all these years and not have heard more about it? I found a copy of the plans with a news comment on it and that they are preserved in Eugene and a well-known Salem architect by the name of W.D. Pugh had drawn them. Why didn't he ever talk about it or take us there? Karen never heard of it and Jerry lived in Eugene, and he didn't know about it, I am sure.

After I found the paper article and saw the pictures, I had a desire to see it, but when it said Skinner's Butte, I thought it was miles away—it is across from the depot, right downtown, perched among the trees across from the R.R. Station. Imagine my surprise when Ramona said that she knew I wanted to see it and that is where we were going, and she drove up to the depot and parked across the street.

They were getting ready for an open house, and there were several ladies hustling about, and I hesitated—she didn't—she marched right in and said she had the architect's daughter outside and could she see it. They ushered me right in and introduced me as the granddaughter of the architect—I would correct them and they would do it again, so I had to have the facts and say my father was 40 years old when I was born and I had had my 92 [birthday]. It was difficult for them to get the picture. They want me to do a short article on him and send it to them for their book, which I will do now that Karen ran off the material they gave me and I found a picture of W.D. holding me. I look about like 8 months, so he must have been around 41, as his [birthday] was April 4th and mine Aug. 1st, 1903.

History bothers and bewilders me because everyone has a different account and a different date.

I have always (since the "Saving of Whitespires") been told it was my father's first architectural venture while he was studying in Portland with the architects McCay [sic] and Wickersham, but the date of the laying of the cornerstone is shown as June 20, 1891. Could they have had the plans for some time trying to raise the funds? This Eugene house says it was designed by a Salem architect W.D. Pugh and was built in 1888. My mother was 8 years old at that time, and he would have been 25, as he was born in 1863. It is a work of art. You must see it some time.

When my father was 17, he won an architectural contest, and a man came out from New York and begged his father to let him go to N.Y., and he wouldn't let him go. Dad never liked Salem; what an opportunity that would have been.

I have a book, *Not on a Silver Platter*, written by a Salem woman a graduate of W.U. [Willamette University] and a friend of your dad's that is all about Salem history. Her grandfather was an early dentist at the same time Dad was in his office downtown.

On page 213, it states that Walter Pugh is going to put up a two-story brick building with an L shape with a frontage on Commercial St. and

Chemeketa at the cost of $7,000.00 and stated that Pugh must be doing well. This apparently was right after the house in Eugene, which you will note cost $7,000.00 to build—an impressive amount of money at that time. On page 293, it mentions that Dr. Meredith went across the hall to Pugh's office to watch them open bids for the Woolen Mills.

Maybe memories were painful to Dad. He had enjoyed prestige, was a state architect during Gov. Penoyer's [sic] term and had made lots of money then decided that his eyes were not as good and decided to work out of [i.e., outside of] his office and be a contractor. He was an artist not a businessman. That turned out to be a disaster, as he had a huge contract to macadamize the highway between Monroe and Harrington WA. Rock crusher and all—a very expensive deal and he had acquired a partner, which [sic] did the book work and absconded with the money that should have paid the bills—leaving the operation in bankruptcy. He had to sell farms, stock, several properties and had nothing left but our house. That is when we came to 18th St. in 1920. He never recovered from that blow, and mother said his pride kept him from ever getting a regular job—He did get some contracts, as he designed and built the Methodist home on Center—Woolen Mills building and poultry barn at the state fairgrounds and etc. But he had a fancy expensive car that cost $3,000.00 when your mother was a very small child—farm with registered stock—two modern homes and a huge barn. One house for the farmer and family who he paid by the month and one for us as a vacation home. We traveled by train with a fancy hunting dog called Stylish Fannie. He loved to hunt pheasants. He was late like your mother? I can remember them holding the train at the depot—the conductor walking up and down looking at his watch while we arrived, dog and all. We live a 3 short blocks away. I can still remember being embarrassed at causing the passengers to wait. Did not bother him, and yet, he was a caring, just person otherwise. Probably the past was painful to him, but I can't imagine him not showing us the house in Eugene because we were in Eugene from time to time.

I better get up and do something, or I will get used to sitting.

Dr. Hoyt, first president of WU married David Hall Pugh and Catharine Entz in 1860. David had taken some classes at the university. It might have been called the Willamette Institute then. He built their house on Winter and Union in 1860 and lived there on 3 lots until he died. I have the deed to the property written by hand on blue stationery. My great grandfather Hobson owned 1,500 acres between Sublimity and Stayton. It was called Hobson's Corner until they were getting a post office and, because of the beautiful view, called it Sublimity, which seemed a better name for a town. You have more history than the Iowa reunion, which will probably stop when your Dad can no longer make the pilgrimage.

I could go on and on, but you must be weary by now.

David and Nancy stopped by yesterday. Karen took me to breakfast Wednesday—family contacts are few now. I miss all the family that used to come up this long walk to the door—maybe not for long—who knows.

Hope you can read this—I remember your mother's reluctance in writing because she was afraid she would make an error—I am not that well educated—I just go at it?

Love,
Auntie

P.S. Hope Joseph gets along o.k. in his independent living venture. We didn't do our children a favor when roast beef and mashed potatoes and gravy gave way to hamburgers and French fries. We lost the family.

NOTES

Chapter 1

1. According to information provided by his grandson and Walter's brother David W. Pugh at David Hall's interment in 1912 ("Pugh Family History—Keizer, Oregon"). One David Pugh, with three unnamed dependents under sixteen, was counted in the 1790 census of South Carolina. In most printed sources, William David Pugh's birth year is given as 1790 (possibly January 3), but L. Heindl, in a detailed, handwritten roster of the Pugh family's member vital statistics, gives his birthdate as February 6, 1785.
2. It was presumably in Indiana that William D. Pugh became involved with the new Protestant denomination Disciples of Christ, which was founded in Kentucky in 1832. No evidence was discovered of any pastoral functions being filled by Pugh Sr.
3. Sarah Hunt Steeves, *Book of Remembrance of Marion County, Oregon, Pioneers 1840–1860* (Portland, OR: Berncliff Press, 1927), as cited in an obituary for David Hall Pugh. (See note 7.)
4. "Descendants of William David Pugh," a genealogical history of the Pugh family, compiled. A copy was provided to the author by Stephenie Flora.
5. According to Mrs. Steeves, in a 1926 interview with Catherine Entz Pugh, David Hall's widow, the older brothers only took part in the Cayuse War in 1855, the year it ended.
6. *Statesman Journal*, December 11, 1912, 1.

7. *Sunday Oregonian,* December 15, 1912, section two, 7. There are many discrepancies on the details of the Pugh family's history in print, including birth and death dates. David Hall's were certainly February 22, 1833, and December 10, 1912

8. Ibid., 46.

9. Demolished in 1935 to make room for the construction of the Oregon State Library. (See photographs.)

10. The course of study for students in the Academical Department included spelling, reading, writing, grammar, geography, arithmetic, composition, U.S. history and "object lessons" (communication of Ariel Valdivia, registrar's office, Willamette University, August 8, 2019).

11. Steeves, *Book of Remembrance,* 233–34. Cited from the chronicler of pioneer experiences in Marion County, Oregon. Steeves's grandparents were managers of the Bennett Hotel at the time of the Entz children's arrival. Her account of a 1926 interview with "little Grandma Pugh" is the only published Pugh family document of its kind discovered at the time of this writing.

12. There is a fair amount of fluctuation in accounts of the Entz family's saga in matters of dates and a few other details.

13. Catharine's journey was surely the more harrowing and hazardous of the two, of course. The Pugh family train is generally thought to have taken the notorious Meek Cutoff across the Malheur Desert of eastern Oregon rather than the by then already established route north, roughly parallel to the Snake River, and then down the Columbia River. (The Meek Cutoff train of 1845, it has been argued, lost more lives than the Donner Party.) However, there is reason to doubt that the Pugh family was part of the Meek train. There appears to be no mention of any Pugh family member in the published diaries and memoirs of Meek survivors, and there is no mention of the Meek Cutoff in Pugh sources. See the reminiscences of one of William Porter Pugh's daughters: Estella Pugh, *Oregon Daily Journal,* April 10, 1936. On the Meek Cutoff, see Keith Clark and Lowell Tiller, *Terrible Trail: The Meek Cutoff, 1845* (Caldwell, ID: Caxton Printers, 1966). The authors put the Pughs in the "believed to have taken the Meek Cutoff" category, along with several other families.

14. "Walter Pugh, Pioneer State Architect, Dies," *Statesman Journal,* November 23, 1946, 1.

15. *Weekly Oregon Statesman,* September 22, 1875. At least part of his education was also done in public schools; see "A Leading Architect," *Statesman Journal,* January 1, 1903, 58.

16. Communication of Ariel Valdivia, registrar's office, Willamette University, August 8, 2019.

17. Ritz, *Architects of Oregon*, 277, 425; Leland Roth and Edward H. Teague, "McCaw, Martin, and White Architects," Oregon Encyclopedia, www.oregonenclyclopedia.com. There is no additional information on Wickersham.

Chapter 2

18. Ritz, *Architects of Oregon*, 47, 235–36.

19. *Weekly Oregon Statesman*, September 26, 1890. Boothby is included in the list of seventy-nine "Muldoons," or those who paid taxes on $10,000 or more in Marion County.

20. The building was designed by the Portland firm of Piper & Burton. It was demolished in 1952.

21. Ritz, *Architects of Oregon*, 47.

22. *Statesman Journal*, April 20, 1912, citing an 1882 book, Frank E. Hodgkin and J.J. Galvin, *Pen Pictures of Representative Men of Oregon* (Portland, OR: Farmer and Dairyman Publishing House, 1882).

23. It should be noted that an obituary in 1912 mentions Boothby's opening of an architect's office, "in which business he is still engaged" (*Statesman Journal*, April 20, 1912, 2).

24. *Statesman Journal*, April 21, 1887, 3.

25. Communication of Dave Hegeman, State Library of Oregon, Government Information and Library Services; Ritz, *Architects of Oregon*, 230–31. Pugh was appointed architect for the county in 1905, in connection with his preparation of the Marion County booth for the Lewis and Clark Exposition, which was held during that centenary year in Portland.

26. *Statesman Journal*, March 18, 1888, 3; *Capital Journal*, March 15, 1894, 3.

27. Whiffen, *American Architecture*, 97–102.

28. *Capital Journal*, June 13, 1891.

29. Communication of Anna Dvorak, Special Collections and Archives Research Center (SCARC), Oregon State University Library, March 11, 2020.

30. Communication of Larry Landis, Special Collections and Archives Research Center (SCARC), October 1, 2019.

31. *Salem Journal*, March 23, 1888, 3; *Morning Oregonian*, July 27, 1888, 3; *Salem Journal*, August 23, 1889, 2; *Salem Journal*, June 7, 1891, 2; *Weekly Oregon Statesman*, February 19, 1892, 12.

32. *Capital Journal*, February 29, 1892; William Allen Bentson, *Historic Capitols of Oregon, An Illustrated Chronology* (Salem, OR: State Library of Oregon, 1987).

33. *Sunday Oregonian*, February 12, 1911, 8; Ritz, *Architects of Oregon*, 236. According to one source, the dome was designed by architect Lionel Deane, who was employed by Krumbein's firm in 1892.

34. *Statesman Journal*, November 24, 1946, 1.

35. Ritz, *Architects of Oregon*, 324.

36. *Corvallis Gazette-Times*, August 8, 1891, 4.

37. Charles H. Burggraf (1866–1942), a near contemporary of W.D. Pugh, was born in Illinois and educated in Nebraska (he was one of the few Oregon architects of his generation to have formally studied engineering). He came to Salem in 1891, then moved to Albany, Oregon, around 1896. He designed a number of buildings in Albany, including the St. Francis Hotel and the public library and two courthouses in Sherman and Wheeler Counties, east of the Cascade Range (1899 and 1902, respectively).

38. Cornelius Sarsfield McNally (1858–1938?) was born in Quebec, educated in Michigan and was an experienced builder-architect when he came to Salem in 1889. In 1893, he moved to the San Francisco Bay Area. In Salem, he designed a number of houses and the Capital National Bank Building, which is listed in the National Register of Historic Places (Ritz, *Architects of Oregon*, 281).

39. *Statesman Journal*, March 23, 1893, 4.

40. Ibid.

41. *Capital Journal*, April 5, 1893.

42. *Statesman Journal*, June 11, 1893.

43. *Capital Journal*, March 27, 1897, 2.

44. *Weekly Oregon Statesman*, June 8, 1895, 5.

45. *Capital Journal*, February 8, 1895.

46. *Statesman Journal*, February 20, 1895, 4.

47. *Statesman Journal*, April 17, 1895, 4.

48. Ibid.

49. Ibid., 1.

50. "The City Hall Is Accepted, and the Officials Will Move in Next Week," *Capital Journal*, March 27, 1897, 2; "Architect's Widow Will Miss City Hall," *Capital Journal*, August 3, 1972, 1.

51. *Capital Journal*, February 8, 1895, 4. The paper later corrected this article, which reported the hiring of Mr. Harrild as a replacement of Pugh as superintending architect. Harrild was hired on as assistant superintending.

52. National Register of Historic Places inventory, nomination form (#84003028), 1.

53. It seems the source of this version of the arson was a "vague note" in a University of Oregon Library publication titled *Call Number* (April 1956). Another version said that the fire was started by a rival architect who was refused the contract. *Eugene Guard*, June 12, 1968, 30.

54. According to the most recent (2010) census, it has narrowly ceded that distinction to Salem. Pugh's floorplans and elevations on silk for the Shelton-McMurphey-Johnson house are preserved in the archive of the Lane County Historical Society, Eugene.

55. Hawkins and Willingham, "Chapter 6." Among McCaw-designed houses were the Thornton house, circa 1885, in Portland, and commanding officer's quarters, 1886, at Fort Vancouver. There are surviving examples of the Queen Anne style to be found around the state, including the Settlemeier mansion in Woodburn and the Drain house in Drain.

56. See appendix A.

57. See appendix A.

58. None of them appear on the "historic sites research list" for Salem and the surrounding area generated by the Oregon Historic Preservation Office.

59. One is the George J. Pearce house on North Winter Street (1892), the present site of the Presbyterian Church. The Gilbert house is another (see appendix A).

60. Dr. S.E. Josephi, a prominent specialist "on nervous diseases and treatment of the insane," was superintendent of the asylum from May 1886 to June 1887. His election of Pugh's services apparently came through that connection.

61. See the timelines by project type in appendix A.

62. *Weekly Oregon Statesman*, September 9, 1887, 6. Neer, who was half a generation older than Pugh (born in 1847), probably set the record for designing Oregon courthouses: Clackamas, Benton, Washington, Lane, Baker and Polk Counties. Several were still in service as of 2002 (Ritz, *Architects of Oregon*, 294).

63. *Morning Oregonian*, October 10, 1888, 3; *Statesman Journal*, March 3, 1888.

64. *Statesman Journal*, May 5, 1888, 2.

65. National Archives Catalog, National Parks Service, record group 79, series: National Register of Historic Places and National Historic Landmarks Program, file: Unit Program Records: Oregon, item: Oregon SP, Salem Downtown, State Street–Commercial Street Historic District.

66. To be exact, 196 feet and 8 inches. Description of the whole is in *Statesman Journal*, March 2, 1889, 4.

67. The northern part, which reached Chemeketa Street and wrapped around, was razed for a parking lot in 1954. The surviving South Eldridge portion of the Eldridge Block, the Greeenbaum Building, has a "local landmark" designation.

68. National Archives Catalog: National Register of Historic Places inventory, nomination forms: Bush-Breyman Block (Breyman portion) (#78002298); Bush-Brey Block (#81000505), Salem, Oregon.

69. Pugh's original design included a sixty-one-foot-tall tower that was not built (National Register of Historic Places inventory, nomination form: Bush-Breyman Block (Breyman Portion), 2).

70. By 1887, Pugh had already designed a two-story brick building with a frontage of forty-nine feet, "just north of the State Insurance Company's building on Commercial Street" (*Weekly Oregon Statesman*, May 27, 1887, 5).

71. William J. Hawkins III, *The Grand Era of Cast-Iron Architecture in Portland* (Portland, OR: Binfords & Mort, 1981).

72. *Statesman Journal*, March 2, 1889, 4.

73. Ladd and Bush Bank Building, located at 302 State Street in Salem and listed in the National Register of Historic Places, was built in 1869. In 1892, Bush had Pugh design a new brick building next to the bank (*Weekly Oregon Statesman*, June 3, 1892, 4).

74. Most of the biographical information is drawn from the National Register of Historic Places, Salem Downtown Historic District, Salem, Oregon. There is considerable literature on Bush, probably the best-known name in Salem history.

75. The block was originally called the Exchange Block. An article in the *Statesman Journal* proposed changing the block's name to Eldridge Block. "Mr. Eldridge, who died only a few days ago, deserved much of the credit for the building of the block, his estate owns a considerable portion of it, and it would be a most appropriate thing to change the name. The Eldridge Block sounds well" (*Statesman Journal*, February 22, 1890).

76. *Statesman Journal*, January 21, 1894.

77. The National Register of Historic Places registration form named Walter D. Pugh and John Gray as architects. Gray was Pugh's associate for several years, mainly on construction projects. The contractors of the Chemeketa Lodge buildings were Erixon and Van Patten.

78. For a photograph of the building exterior as it was designed, see page 52.

79. *Statesman Journal*, July 1, 1892, 1; *Statesman Journal*, August 14, 1892, 4.

80. *Capital Journal*, April 4, 1890, 4.

81. *Capital Journal*, June 4, 1891, 3.

82. *Statesman Journal*, November 19, 1895, 5; *Statesman Journal*, August 2, 1889, 2. The August 9 edition of *Statesman Journal* stated that bids were opened on August 8. It seems that in the end, the dimensions were 136 by 55 feet.

83. *Statesman Journal*, August 16, 1889, 4.

84. *Statesman Journal*, November 19, 1895, 5.

85. "He was married in 1857, three days before his departure for America. He and his estimable wife have six children living, four dead" (*Weekly Oregon Statesman*, January 3, 1890, 1).

86. Ibid.

87. Alfred L. Lomax, "Thomas Kay Woolen Mill Co., A Family Enterprise," *Oregon Historical Quarterly* 54, no. 2 (June 1953): 106. As quoted in "Historic American Buildings Survey: Thomas Kay Woolen Mill Buildings (1969)"; a mimeographed copy was provided by Elisabeth Walton Potter. To prepare for the construction of his mill, Kay toured the mills of New England and England to learn about the latest machines and processes that were then in use.

88. *Weekly Oregon Statesman*, January 3, 1890, 1. This long piece contains interesting biographical and professional details about Thomas Kay.

89. However, the press reported that the plans for the new mill were then complete and could be examined, along with specifications, in the office of W.D. Pugh in the Tioga Block on December 21 only, and an invitation for bids on the foundation work of the new mill went out from Pugh's office on December 26. Bids were to be opened on December 28 (*Capital Journal*, December 21, 1895, 5; *Capital Journal*, December 26, 1895, 4).

90. *Capital Journal*, December 21, 1895, 5; *Capital Journal*, December 26, 1895, 4.

91. *Statesman Journal*, December 6, 1895, 5.

92. *Statesman Journal*, May 12, 1904, 4.

93. National Park Service, National Register of Historic Places, nomination form no. 86003182, address: 302 South Main Street, Independence, Oregon.

94. *Morning Register* (Eugene, OR), June 8, 1902, 4.

95. *Eugene Guard*, December 16, 1902, 1; *Morning Register*, December 16, 1902, 6.

96. *Statesman Journal*, June 18, 1901, 7. The Soldiers' Home was originally created for aged Civil War veterans.

97. *Roseburg Review*, April 8, 1905, 1. There were, in fact, several discrete indictments, but they were all for conspiring to defraud the government

of land. James Henry Booth was also charged with leaking advance information while he was a receiver of the government land office.

Chapter 3

98. *Capital Journal*, June 29, 1911, 6; *Statesman Journal*, June 29, 1911, 6.

99. *Statesman Journal*, June 19, 1897, 4; *Weekly Oregon Statesman*, June 25, 1897, 3; *Capital Journal*, November 3, 1897, 4. One of the reports noted that Hunsaker's annual tax bill was $6.97.

100. *Capital Journal*, November 3, 1897, 4

101. *Capital Journal*, January 27, 1898, 3.

102. *Eugene Guard*, August 8, 1899, 1; *Eugene Guard*, February 24, 1900.

103. *Statesman Journal*, February 27, 1900, 5.

104. Pugh did provide designs for some additions and alterations to a dormitory at the university in 1903; around the same time, he was submitting plans for a new high school in Eugene (*Statesman Journal*, April 8, 1903, 5).

105. *Capital Journal*, November 23, 1896, 4.

106. *Capital Journal*, September 3, 1896, 4.

107. *Weekly Oregon Statesman*, July 9, 1897, 8.

108. *Eugene Guard*, May 31, 1897, 1; *Eugene Guard*, February 16, 1898, 4.

109. *Statesman Journal*, July 2, 1897, 1.

110. *Statesman Journal*, March 17, 1898, 8.

111. *Statesman Journal*, March 25, 1898, 5.

112. *Weekly Oregon Statesman*, December 23, 1898, 3. The Capital Grounds and Building Commission of Arizona Territory had begun advertising in the local press for plans and cost estimates for a capitol building in the spring of 1898. Pugh may well have entered a bid. By November, the commission had selected an architect, J.R. Gordon, and specifications and details were to be made ready for bidders on December 12 (*Arizona Republican*, November 19, 1898, 4). The building was completed in August 1900 by building contractor Tom Lovell of Texas.

113. *Statesman Journal*, May 30, 1899, 8.

114. *Capital Journal*, June 19, 1899, 3; *Statesman Journal*, June 24, 1899, 6.

115. *Eugene Guard*, 5 August 1899, 1.

116. The Siletz buildings "on the hill" have all been demolished. Those that were constructed by Pugh were probably the hospital and the dormitory/dining hall (see appendix A); T. Jay Buford, Siletz agent, reports to the commissioner of Indian affairs, 1899, 1900, copies provided by Peter

Hatch; "Messrs. Grey [*sic*] and Pugh, of Salem, arrived last evening. These gentlemen have the contract to build the boarding school kitchen at the agency. Two car-loads of lumber arrived the first of the week and will be hauled over as rapidly as possible" (*Lincoln County Leader*, August 25, 1899); communication of Tammy Wild with the author; *Oregonian*, October 1, 1901, 4. The bricks for Chemawa were supplied by Pugh's uncle Silas George Pugh, who had a brickyard on his land claim at Keizer that "included part of Lake Labish and the clay banks above the lake."

117. *Statesman Journal*, November 8, 1901.

118. *Capital Journal*, March 15, 1899, 5; *Capital Journal*, December 31, 1897, 5. Gray and his wife attend a New Year's social that was given by the school pupils.

119. "Architect W.D. Pugh and Chas. A. Gray were in Woodburn on Wednesday Afternoon," *Capital Journal*, December 23, 1897, 5; *Capital Journal*, November 10, 1897, 4.

120. *Capital Journal*, May 12, 1900, 3; *Capital Journal*, May 16, 1900, 3; *Capital Journal*, June 4, 1900, 3.

121. *Oregon Daily Journal* (Portland), July 5, 1902, 2; *Oregon Daily Journal*, November 21, 1902, 5.

122. *Oregon Daily Journal*, April 22, 1903, 8.

123. *Oregon Daily Journal* (Portland), April 15, 1908, 10.

124. *Statesman Journal*, June 29, 1911, 6. While in Salem, the article continues, he was "deeply interested in assisting released convicts to obtain employment and become useful citizens."

125. *Oregonian*, August 22, 1915, 14.

126. *Statesman Journal*, January 2, 1906, 19. "Fred A. Legg has become a partner of Mr. Pugh and the firm Pugh & Legg."

127. One brief notice in the *Capital Journal* (March 15, 1899), "Chas. A. Gray, supervising architect of the new assembly hall at Chemawa, came up today," suggests otherwise, but the function was probably assumed from the architectural credentials.

128. When "Architect W.D. Pugh and wife came up [to Waterloo] from Salem on their wheels" in August 1895, they had most likely brought their "wheels" (bicycles) with them on the train to Lebanon, which is six and a half miles from Waterloo. Touring in the countryside with bicycles brought by train was apparently quite popular in the valley in the late nineteenth century.

129. The authority on early Oregon railroads is Edwin D. Culp's *Stations West*. It includes many timetables. The concisely informative "Railroading

in the Lower Willamette Valley," an online contribution to the Horner Museum Tour Guide Series, Benton County Museum (1979), by Robert Lowry, Kenneth Munford and Harriet Moore, is very useful. Also, Randall V. Mills's *Railroads Down the Valley* is informative on this subject.

130. *Statesman Journal*, August 13, 1885, 3.

131. Fannie E. Rhodes (September 8, 1868–September 27, 1901).

132. *Statesman Journal*, May 1, 1886, 3. Inez Pugh Cable (March 20, 1886–February 8, 1971).

133. Allen E. Pugh (May 12, 1888–April 13, 1953); Albert W. Pugh (January 3, 1891–November 1, 1918).

134. *Capital Journal*, August 20, 1895, 3.

135. *Capital Journal*, June 19, 1899, 3; *Statesman Journal*, June 24, 1899, 6 (citing a story in the *Phoenix Herald* from June 9, 1899).

136. *Capital Journal*, September 21, 1901, 4; *Capital Journal*, September 27, 1901, 4.

137. *Statesman Journal*, September 28, 1901, 6.

138. *Oregonian*, October 1, 1901, 4.

139. *Oregonian*, March 2, 1902, 20.

140. *Statesman Journal*, February 26, 1902, 6.

141. Terence Emmons, ed., "Hadley Hobson Marion County Pioneer," *Oregon Historical Quarterly* 93, no.1 (Spring 1992): 65–73.

142. "Architect's Widow Will Miss City Hall," *Capital Journal*, August 3, 1972, 1.

Chapter 4

143. "Illustrated Annual 1903," *Statesman Journal*, 58.

144. *Morning Register*, December 16, 1902, 6. "Opera house" was the general designation for a building that was meant for a variety of theatrical purposes. They usually had stages, orchestra pits, audience seating and backstage facilities for costumes and sets in the precinematic age. As a rule, they became movie theaters later, much of the variety having disappeared in smaller cities and towns.

145. *Eugene Guard*, January 30, 1903, 3. No satisfactory photograph of the opera house's façade could be found.

146. Information provided by the Oregon Theater Project.

147. Maurice Klinger, a former brewer and saloonkeeper. The building contained a small variety theater, the Edison (*Statesman Journal*, May 1,

1902, 5; *Statesman Journal*, July 9, 1902, 5; *Capital Journal*, July 22, 1902, 3; *Weekly Oregon Statesman*, February 6, 1903, 7).

148. *Weekly Oregon Statesman*, March 27, 1903, 7.

149. *Capital Journal*, April 15, 1903, 3.

150. *Capital Journal*, June 5, 1903, 6.

151. *Oregon Daily Journal* (Portland), January 23, 1904, 4.

152. *Statesman Journal*, April 8, 1903, 5; *Weekly Oregon Statesman*, March 27, 1903, 7.

153. *Statesman Journal*, February 28, 1904, 4.

154. *Capital Journal*, March 14, 1904, 3.

155. *Weekly Oregon Statesman*, December 30, 1904, 5. In early 1905, Carey was working for Legg on plans for the new school for the deaf.

156. *Capital Journal*, August 27, 1938, 10.

157. *Statesman Journal*, January 1, 1903, 35.

158. *Capital Journal*, April 18, 1899, 4.

159. *Capital Journal*, May 4, 1899, 4.

160. *Statesman Journal*, July 27, 1897, 8.

161. "*Statesman Journal*, June 4, 1911, 15. The 1938 article on Carey listed the early 1909 Legg plans for the deaf-mute school as Carey's handiwork as well.

162. *Statesman Journal*, December 4, 1910, 19.

163. *Weekly Oregon Statesman*, January 24, 1905, 7; *Statesman Journal*, July 6, 1929, 7.

164. *Weekly Oregon Statesman*, January 24, 1905, 7.

165. *Statesman Journal* Blog, "Salem High School," January 4, 2014, www.statesmanjournal.com.

166. *Statesman Journal*, January 2, 1906, 19.

167. Ibid.

168. *Weekly Oregon Statesman*, April 28, 1905, 3.

169. Steven Robert Heine, *The Oregon State Fair* (Charleston, SC: Arcadia Publishing, 2007), 40; *Capital Journal*, January 1, 1910, 23.

170. *Capital Journal*, December 19, 1905, 4.

171. *Weekly Oregon Statesman*, May 16, 1905, 8.

172. "Report of the Lewis and Clark Centennial Exposition Commission for the State of Oregon. Held at Portland, Oregon, June First to October Fifteenth, Nineteen Hundred and Five," scanned copy provided by Oregon State Library.

173. *Statesman Journal*, October 15, 1905, 3.

174. *Statesman Journal*, April 13, 1905, 4.

175. "Fred Legg, the Architect, who Has Opened an Office in the Ainsworth Building in Portland, Returned to the Metropolis [Salem] After a Brief Over-Sunday Visit with His Family," *Capital Journal*, October 15, 1906, 8; "Fred A. Legg, the Portland Architect, Is in Salem on Business," *Statesman Journal*, September 10, 1907, 4.

176. Typically, this was a sizeable two-story building (one hundred by sixty-five feet), with income-producing shops below and the fraternal lodge above.

177. As recorded in *Portland Daily Abstract*.

178. *Statesman Journal*, August 27, 1905, 4.

179. Charles A. Howard, "A History of High School Education in Oregon to 1910," *Quarterly of the Oregon Historical Society* 24, no. 3 (September 1923): 227–29.

180. *Capital Journal*, May 5, 1905, 4.

181. *Capital Journal*, July 19, 1905, 4. A finance committee meeting was held at the office of Dean Byrd in the opera building. The committee had succeeded in raising about $12,000 in a subscription campaign.

182. Ibid.

183. Gatke Hall is older, but it is a former post office building that moved to campus in 1938.

184. Salem Online History, provided by Salem Public Library and Willamette University. (It may be recalled that the architect's parents had once attended the academy, originally known as the Oregon Institute.)

185. Wikipedia, "Art Building (Willamette University)," www.wikipedia.com.

186. National Park Service, National Register of Historic Places inventory, nomination form: Benton County State Bank Building (Second and Madison Streets, Corvallis, Oregon, no. 77848700).

187. *Portland Daily Abstracts*, 394–96 (index; summary three, buildings sorted by names of architect/designers, numbers in [-] are entry dates).

188. Hawkins and Willingham, *Classic Houses*.

189. *Capital Journal*, March 20, 1907, 2.

190. *Statesman Journal*, May 26, 1907, 3.

191. *Statesman Journal*, July 17, 1907, 3. Legg did design a building for Fairview, a girls' dormitory (Smith Cottage), but long after their partnership had ended, in 1921.

192. Wikipedia, "Fairview Training Center," www.wikipedia.com.

193. *Statesman Journal*, March 11, 1908, 1.

194. Sara Glaser, "Erasing Fairview's Horrors," *Oregon Live*, last updated, January 10, 2019.

195. *Morning Register*, 28 April 1908, 8.

196. *Statesman Journal*, February 21, 1908, 3.

197. Oregon Encyclopedia, "Crook County Courthouse," www.oregonencyclopedia.org

198. Ibid.

199. Lent, *Crook County Courthouse*, 5.

200. Ibid., 1.

201. Culp, *Stations West*, 128.

202. David Braly, "Central Oregon's Best-Known Building," in *Little Known Tales from Oregon History: A Collection of 23 Stories from Cascades East Magazine*, vol. 3 (Bend, OR: Sun Publishers, 2001).

203. *Statesman Journal*, May 19, 1908, 7.

204. *Statesman Journal*, June 12, 1908.

205. Ibid.

206. *Statesman Journal*, January 1, 1909, 31.

207. *Statesman Journal*, May 19, 1909, 7.

208. *Statesman Journal*, May 30, 1909.

209. *Statesman Journal*, June 11, 1909, 5.

210. *Capital Journal*, June 12, 1909, 6.

211. *Statesman Journal*, November 15, 1908, 7. It may be noted that several members of the Herren family had been on the 1845 St. Joseph Company wagon train along with the Pughs.

212. *Statesman Journal*, December 27, 1908, 10; *Statesman Journal*, March 4, 1909, 1–2.

213. *Statesman Journal*, September 26, 1909, 1.

214. *Statesman Journal*, January 1, 1910, 2.

215. *Capital Journal*, January 1, 1910, 23.

216. *Capital Journal*, April 16, 1909, 2.

Chapter 5

217. *Capital Journal*, March 17, 1910, 1.

218. *Capital Journal*, March 27, 1911, 2.

219. *Capital Journal*, February 22, 1912, 5.

220. *Statesman Journal*, June 9, 1922, 1.

221. In a session in May 1910, the Salem City Council debated a proposal to tax automobiles ten dollars to defray the cost of sprinkling the streets to keep down dust (*Capital Journal*, May 24, 1910, 4).

222. *Statesman Journal*, April 25, 1909, 6; *Statesman Journal*, August 21, 1910, 11.

223. *Capital Journal*, June 24, 1913, 3. (See appendix A.)

224. *Albany Evening Herald*, April 27, 1911, 1.

225. *Capital Journal*, April 11, 1913.

226. *Statesman Journal*, September 27, 1910, 5–6.

227. *Capital Journal*, September 27, 1910, 5.

228. *Capital Journal*, May 17, 1913, 1.

229. *Capital Journal*, May 27, 1913, 1, 4.

230. *Oregonian*, July 22, 1910, 2.

231. *Statesman Journal*, July 22, 1910, 1.

232. *Capital Journal*, May 21, 1912, 9; *Capital Journal*, May 22, 1912, 4.

233. *Statesman Journal*, May 22, 1912, 8.

234. *Capital Journal*, May 20, 1912, 1. See the online database of labor-related events in 1912 "I.W.W. Yearbook: 1912," which was derived from the "Industrial Worker," University of Washington, IWW History Project (online).

235. William L. White, "Franchising Addiction Treatment: The Keeley Institutes," in *Slaying the Dragon: the History of Addiction Treatment and Recovery in America* (Bloomington, IL: Chestnut Health Systems/Lighthouse Institute, 1998). The evidence in question comes from a report in the January 11, 1894 edition of the *Statesman Journal*. It reported on the regular meeting of the "Keeley League" the previous evening, when the following officers were elected: president, W.D. Pugh; vice president, Ed. N. Edes, etc. The Keeley Leagues were organized by "graduates" of the "Keeley method" of treatment, which included a course of injections of dubious efficacy for alcoholism, drug addiction, "for tobacco (all forms) and for Neurasthenia or nerve exhaustion" (*Statesman Journal*, January 10, 1897, 4). The Keeley Leagues were administered by the Keeley Institute of Dwight, Illinois, and its franchises, which sprang up around the country in the 1890s. The Keeley Leagues were predecessors of Alcoholics Anonymous (AA) to the extent that the Keeley method was based on the disease theory of addiction. But unlike AA, they were not anonymous; names of officers were published in the newspapers, and they organized entertainment events for which tickets were sold to the general public.

236. Samuel Sloan, *City and Suburban Architecture; Containing Numerous Designs and Details for Public Edifices, Private Residences, and Mercantile Buildings. Illustrated with One Hundred and Thirty-Six Engravings. Accompanied by Specifications and Historical and Explanatory Text* (Philadelphia: J.P. Lippincott, 1859, 1867). Sloan also published guides for houses, cottages, farmhouses and even banks.

237. Jerry Lomas, personal communication with the author.

238. Deed record no. 52, Polk County, warranty deed no. 949.
239. *Statesman Journal*, July 27, 1913, 4.
240. *Capital Journal*, December 30, 1911, 23.
241. Deed record no. 60, Polk County, warranty deed no. 7374.
242. Was this the lot on North Eighteenth Street where he built a house for his family in 1921?
243. Marion county clerk's office records, "Pugh, W.D., and Jessie Hobson," dated October 3, 1902; October 11, 1902; October 20, 1902; May 7, 1903; sums ranging from $1,400 to $2,600.
244. *Capital Journal*, September 16, 1905, 7.
245. Warranty deed on file in Lincoln County, Oregon, clerk's office, document 334148973131353.pdf.
246. *Statesman Journal*, November 15, 1908, 7.
247. *Statesman Journal*, March 4, 1909, 2; *Statesman Journal*, August 31, 1909, 1; *Capital Journal*, August 6, 1909, 8.
248. *Statesman Journal*, April 9, 1913, 4.
249. The Herren party endured the notorious Meek Cutoff. There seems to be no reliable evidence that the Pugh party took it, despite their presence (albeit, with a cautionary asterisk) on the list of families in the principal monograph on the Meek Cutoff (Clark and Tiller, *Terrible Trail*).
250. *Statesman Journal*, March 29, 1913, 5.
251. *Statesman Journal*, August 8, 1913, 4.
252. *Statesman Journal*, October 15, 1913, 5; *Aberdeen Herald*, May 22, 1914, 8.
253. *Aberdeen Herald*, October 27, 1914, 7.
254. *Aberdeen Herald*, November 3, 1914, 4.
255. *Statesman Journal*, January 6, 1915, 5.
256. *Capital Journal*, March 10, 1915, 2.
257. Polk County warranty deed no. 7922 (W.D. Pugh et ux to Alvah Prosser et ux). There may be similar transactions of property in Marion County. Unfortunately, Marion County has not digitized its historical warranty deeds, and the clerk's office is closed to the public at present due to the coronavirus pandemic.
258. Volume 36, deeds, "Alva Prosser & Wife to Jessie H. Pugh," transcript from Crook County, filed October 11, 1915, 447. Thanks to Jeff Sageser of the Deschutes County clerk's office.
259. Tract Index, Deschutes County, Oregon, tp. 15, R. 11; "Jessie H. Pugh & W.D. Pugh to Lemuel Hobson," no. 4091, transcript from Deschutes County, filed April 20, 1918. By 1922, with the Pughs back in Salem and the threat of attachment apparently over, the Sisters property was deeded

back to Jessie Pugh by her father. Finally, Jessie sold the property to John W. Farleigh et ux in 1932.

260. Deed record no. 60, Polk County warranty deed no. 7374.

261. *Statesman Journal*, October 17, 1926, 7.

262. "Alvah Prosser and Wife Arrived in Eugene Last Night from Sisters," *Eugene Guard*, August 27, 1912, 3. The "appurtenances" may be one or both of the two small wooden houses that are still standing on the property.

263. *Capital Journal*, March 12, 1912; *Statesman Journal*, December 13, 1913, 2. There had been an earlier incident of allegations of skimping on thickness of concrete paving.

264. *Oregon Daily Journal*, January 8, 1918, 2.

265. *Oregon Daily Journal*, March 27, 1920, 5; *Oregon Daily Journal*, April 24, 1920, 2.

266. *Oregon Daily Journal*, January 16, 1921, 10.

267. *Oregon Daily Journal*, September 1, 1921, 18.

268. *Morning Register* (Eugene, OR), June 14, 1927, 1.

269. *Capital Journal*, May 14, 1929, 1.

270. *Statesman Journal*, July 27, 1930, 1.

271. *Medford Mail Tribune*, January 7, 1930, 4; *Capital Journal*, June 27, 1935, 1.

272. *Capital Journal*, August 23, 1916, 2.

273. *Bend Bulletin*, November 17, 1917, 2.

274. *Bend Bulletin*, January 16, 1918, 4.

275. *Statesman Journal*, November 8, 1918, 3.

276. *Statesman Journal*, May 29, 1915, 5; *Statesman Journal*, November 8, 1918, 3.

277. *Bend Bulletin*, July 26, 1919, 1.

278. "Oregon Inventory," local I.D. no. 57, Deschutes County, February 3, 1998, www. deschutes.org. "Significant Designers, Contractors & Trades People." (Olson is not identified as "architect" anywhere.)

279. *Bend Bulletin*, August 14, 1919, 3.

280. *Statesman Journal*, August 21, 1921, 5; *Capital Journal*, September 30, 1921, 2.

281. *Capital Journal*, September 1, 1921, 3; *Capital Journal*, April 4, 1922, 3.

282. *Capital Journal*, May 17, 1922, 8.

283. *Statesman Journal*, June 9, 1922, 1.

284. *Statesman Journal*, June 9, 1922, 1.

285. *Statesman Journal*, June 1, 1924, 9.

286. *Statesman Journal*, June 25, 1925, 7.

287. *Capital Journal*, May 12, 1927, 7; *Statesman Journal*, August 6, 1940, 5.

288. *Capital Journal*, May 16, 1928, 7.

289. *Capital Journal*, December 31, 1929, 7; *Statesman Journal*, May 21, 1929, 1.
290. *Capital Journal*, October 16, 1928, 8; *Capital Journal*, December 27, 1928, 1.
291. *Capital Journal*, February 3, 1934, 8; *Capital Journal*, May 19, 1934, 3.
292. *Statesman Journal*, July 26, 1932, 5. And they were still in Idaho in late January 1933, when they received a telegram from the Emmonses about the birth of their first child, David.
293. *Statesman Journal*, July 28, 1936, 5.
294. *Statesman Journal*, September 18, 1937, 5. Monroe is located halfway between Corvallis and Eugene on the west side of the Willamette River.
295. *Statesman Journal*, February 26, 1942, 6.
296. "*Capital Journal*, April 5, 1943.
297. *Statesman Journal*, November 23, 1946, 1. An additional paragraph goes on to describe his education, including time at Willamette University and architectural training during his apprenticeship with McCaw (misspelled McCall) & Wickersham.

Conclusion

298. Anyone who reads the newspapers of the time will notice that the term *capitalist* was regularly used—not as a pejorative but simply as a term for persons with capital to invest.
299. Pugh's work in Portland may be underrepresented here, and the concentration of the firm's commercial projects in the years 1907 and 1908 may be somewhat distorted by the availability of searchable data for the *Portland Daily Abstract* between 1906 and 1909 (and for those years only). No attempt has been made to track Legg's work outside of the partnership.
300. The state historic preservation offices were created by legislation in 1966, but it seems that the active process of making nominations to the register only got underway in the 1980s and 1990s.

SOURCES AND REFERENCE WORKS

Most of W.D. Pugh's buildings were constructed before the introduction of planning or building departments in Oregon's towns and cities. As can be seen from the notes, principal sources for this attempt to catalogue his buildings were local newspapers, especially, but by no means exclusively, as they had announcements calling for bids on construction projects. Fortunately for the researcher, many of these papers have been digitized and adapted for keyword searches. Note: dates assigned to the buildings in this book are more often than not the dates of these announcements for projects that were completed somewhat later. Among the most useful resources for online access to these old Oregon newspapers are:

Historic Oregon Newspapers: A digital collection of 274 titles that is maintained by the Oregon Digital Newspapers Program at the University of Oregon. It is supplemented by the very useful Historic Oregon Newspapers Online by County, a list of Oregon newspapers that are not included in the program but accessible online.

Newspapers.com is a subscription service owned by Ancestry.com. It has a large, digitized repertoire of historical Oregon newspapers with convenient search options.

The mostly vintage photographs of W.D. Pugh's buildings that are reproduced in this book were found in a variety of collections, from city and county historical museums and historical societies; to the Oregon Historical Society; to city, state and university libraries and their archives in Oregon, of course, but also as far as Washington, California, Arizona and New York. Especially useful for searching online resources, including photographs, was the website Oregon Digital, which is jointly managed by the libraries of the University of Oregon and Oregon State University; it provides access to scores of online collections. Of particular importance for the history of architecture among those collections is Building Oregon: Architecture of Oregon and the Pacific Northwest, "with special emphasis on Oregon's historic sites and built environments." For digital photographs of Salem architecture, the Salem Public Library Historic Photograph Collections is unparalleled. Outstanding digital collections of historic photographs of Oregon are also held by the Oregon Historical Society and the State of Oregon Library.

Among many published works consulted, the following were especially useful for this inquiry:

Corning, Howard McKinley, ed. *Dictionary of Oregon History*. Portland, OR: Binfords & Mort, 1956.

Culp, Edwin D. *Stations West: The Story of the Oregon Railways*. Caldwell, ID: Caxton Printers, 1972.

Hawkins, William J., III, and William F. Willingham. *Classic Houses of Portland, Oregon, 1850–1950*. Portland, OR: Timber Press, 1999.

Hines, Gustavus. *Oregon and Its Institutions, Comprising a Full History of the Willamette University, the First Established on the Pacific Coast*. First printed, New York: Carlton & Porter, 1868. Reprint, London: Forgotten Books: 2012.

Lent, Steve, ed. *Crook County Courthouse, Prineville, Oregon: A Documentary History Celebrating 100th Anniversary, 1909–2009*. Prineville, OR: Crook County Historical Society, 2009.

Lomax, Alfred L. *Later Woolen Mills in Oregon*. Portland, OR: Binfords & Mort, 1974.

Lowry, Robert, et al. "Railroading in the Lower Willamette Valley (1979)." www.bentoncountymuseum.org.

McArthur, Lewis A. *Oregon Geographic Names*. 6th ed. revised and enlarged by Lewis L. McArthur. First printed, 1928. Portland: Oregon Historical Society Press, 1992.

Mills, Randall V. *Railroads Down the Valley: Some Short Lines of the Oregon Country*. Palo Alto, CA: Pacific Books, 1950.

Ritz, Richard Ellison. *Architects of Oregon: A Biographical Dictionary of Architects Deceased: 19th and 20th Centuries*. Portland, OR: Lair Hill Publishers, 2002.

Vaughan, Thomas, and Virginia Guest Ferriday, eds. *Space, Style, and Structure: Building in Northwest America*. 2 vols. Portland: Oregon Historical Society Press, 1974.

Whiffen, Marcus. *American Architecture Since 1780: A Guide to the Styles*. Cambridge, MA: MIT Press, 1985.

ABOUT THE AUTHOR

Terence Emmons is a fourth-generation Oregonian. He attended Reed College, the University of Washington (BA) and University of California, Berkeley (MA and PhD), and he was a history professor at Stanford University for many years before retiring to the Applegate Valley. He is the author of several books, including *The Formation of Political Parties and the First National Elections in Russia* and *Alleged Sex and Threatened Violence: The Russians in San Francisco, 1887–1892.*

High School graduation, Albany, Oregon, 1955. Pictured is the author with his grandmother Jessie Hobson Pugh and his parents, Mildred Irene Pugh and Clarence Scott Emmons. *Courtesy of the author.*

Visit us at
www.historypress.com